STRATEGIES
for
TEACHING STUDENTS
with
LEARNING DISABILITIES

STRATEGIES
for
TEACHING STUDENTS
with
LEARNING DISABILITIES

LUCY C. MARTIN

CORWIN PRESS
A SAGE Company

For information:

Corwin Press
A SAGE Company
2455 Teller Road
Thousand Oaks,
  California 91320
www.corwinpress.com

SAGE India Pvt. Ltd.
B 1/I 1 Mohan Cooperative
  Industrial Area
Mathura Road, New Delhi 110 044
India

SAGE Ltd.
1 Oliver's Yard
55 City Road
London EC1Y 1SP
United Kingdom

SAGE Asia-Pacific
  Pte. Ltd.
33 Pekin Street #02-01
Far East Square
Singapore 048763

Printed in the United States of America

Library of Congress Cataloging-in-Publication Data

Martin, Lucy C.
Strategies for teaching students with learning disabilities/Lucy C. Martin.
    p. cm.
Includes bibliographical references and index.
ISBN 978-1-4129-6802-7 (cloth)
ISBN 978-1-4129-6803-4 (pbk.)
    1. Learning disabled children—Education (Elementary)—United States. 2. Learning disabled teenagers—Education (Secondary)—United States. I. Title.

LC4704.73.M35 2009
371.9'0472—dc22   2008034485

This book is printed on acid-free paper.

08 09 10 11 12   10 9 8 7 6 5 4 3 2 1

Acquisitions Editor:	David Chao
Editorial Assistant:	Brynn Saito
Production Editor:	Amy Schroller
Copy Editor:	Melinda Masson
Typesetter:	C&M Digitals (P) Ltd.
Proofreader:	Wendy Jo Dymond
Cover Designer:	Michael Dubowe

Contents

* Includes forms and/or guides

---

* Includes forms and/or guides

---

* Includes forms and/or guides

---

* Includes forms and/or guides

---

* Includes forms and/or guides

* Includes forms and/or guides

---

* Includes forms and/or guides

Acknowledgments

I have learned about teaching from many people. That is a great understatement. The knowledge I have accumulated is the result of having known many wonderful students, teachers, specialists, administrators, and parents. In addition, the concept of sharing was nurtured by generous friends and colleagues, as well as a school climate that brought out the best in me.

I am indebted to many extraordinary people. Without their support, vision, encouragement, and humor, this book would not have been possible. My friends, family, and Corwin Press believed in me and what I had to say. My special thanks go to Darren Ford, Becky Walker, and the McDonogh School. Nearly every student I have known has affected me in some way. Some have inspired me. Thank you, Michael, Jake, and a brilliant, creative young writer who might wish to go unnamed.

About the Author

 **Lucy C. Martin** has been involved in education in a variety of capacities. Her experience includes serving as a resource teacher at public elementary schools in Cambridge, Massachusetts, and Fairfax, Virginia. As educational director of Chesapeake Psychological Services of Maryland (now the Chesapeake ADHD Center of Maryland), she evaluated students with various educational profiles and developed a pamphlet of practical information for classroom teachers working with students who have attention-deficit/hyperactivity disorder (ADHD). At an independent school outside Washington, D.C., she continued to use her clinical and practical expertise as an administrator of students in kindergarten through fifth grade. She currently works as a learning specialist at the McDonogh School outside Baltimore, where she founded a program of support for students with learning disabilities. Beyond teaching students, she has given numerous presentations for parents, educators, and administrators at the local, regional, and national level, including "Finding the Value in Evaluations," "Helping ADHD Students in the Classroom," "Helping Your Child Get Organized for Success at School," and "Creative Map Study." She strives to help classroom teachers understand students with learning disabilities and to offer practical solutions that will work for all students. She advises teachers to see the difference between a "can't" and a "won't." At the core of her approach are personal connections, encouragement, and a belief in a child's best. She often encourages "finding the gift."

Introduction

My first job was that of a "resource teacher." I was flattered but uncomfortable with the title. Despite my formal education, I felt that I had few resources upon which to draw to address day-to-day challenges. With enthusiasm and a relatively empty bag in hand, I began teaching.

In subsequent positions with varied titles and responsibilities, I gained experience but became more aware of the need to expand my bag of tricks. I wanted to have more strategies and tips on organization and a clearer vision of programs. Thankfully, I taught many years alongside skillful educators with encouragement from wise administrators. The students kept me on my toes and inspired me to develop creative solutions to their challenges. Gradually, my bag started to fill to contain many practical suggestions, as well as the wit and wisdom of a seasoned professional. It became the book I had been searching for over many years, and I will unpack it here.

Today, when people ask about my responsibilities as a "learning specialist," I respond that I am a "helper." Each fall, I bring my bag to school in excited anticipation of the experiences that will continue to expand it.

Most educators have enormous responsibilities but little time and limited resources. I've tried to make my suggestions in a direct, to-the-point, jargon-free, and user-friendly way with a bit of humor thrown in for good measure. I hope readers will find this book enjoyable and informative.

Open the bag and enjoy!

1 Awareness and Sensitivity

The Starting Point

The important work of education involves connecting students and teachers in a meaningful way. This connection enables learning to take place. In addition, a deep connection leads to such outcomes as mutual respect and appreciation. Understanding is at the core of this connection. Teachers have many responsibilities, but perhaps their most important responsibility is to understand their students.

Exactly what is involved in understanding a student? A teacher can increase his or her understanding of a student in many ways. Meeting with the student's previous teachers can offer valuable information. The child's cumulative file may contain important communications from parent conferences, as well as a quick overview of success and challenges represented by report cards. If the student is a good listener; speaks effectively, candidly, and comfortably; and has formed a positive association with a former teacher, meeting with him or her can prove useful. Arranging for the learning specialist to observe the student in several classes can help those involved "see" various situations that challenge the student. Finally, while time consuming and expensive in the private sector, an evaluation can offer the most complete and detailed information about a child's learning strengths and challenges. Evaluations come in a number of forms with a variety of titles, including psychoeducational evaluations, psychological evaluations, speech and language evaluations, and so on. Learning disabilities are often diagnosed through a psychoeducational evaluation.

The diagnosis of learning disabilities or attention-deficit/hyperactivity disorder (ADHD) helps a teacher know why a child performs differently from his peers. The diagnosis explains lagging performance in an area of learning, whether academic or social. Understanding why a student has difficulties is the beginning of awareness. For example, a student might have trouble with history for a number of reasons; however, knowing that a student has difficulty with auditory memory can be the beginning of coming to grips with the challenge. Certain types of difficulties, such as anxiety, can masquerade as others, such as ADHD. In this instance, the child may be so preoccupied with internal issues and fears that his attention at school is obscured. Clearly, finding a highly qualified diagnostician is critical to getting the correct "read" on a student who faces obstacles at school.

Still, an intellectual understanding of differences is not enough. Teachers will have the most positive effect when they are sensitive to those differences and their impact on general learning. Relating to students on an emotional level is essential for full understanding. Teachers who can empathize with the challenge of disabilities are in the best position to seek solutions and to share their knowledge and understanding with others. Successful teachers understand their students. If the teacher has no personal experience with a specific learning problem, he or she will have difficulty appreciating its impact on a child's learning and self-esteem in school.

A number of simulation exercises can help demonstrate the obstacles faced at school by students with learning disabilities and ADHD. The feelings associated with these hurdles can be powerful. If a teacher is working with a student who has a type of learning disability that is challenging to understand, it will be important to arrange a meeting with the learning specialist at the school. In addition, seeking opportunities for professional development can allow professionals to truly appreciate the difficulties students face. Rick Lavoie (1989) became well known in the world of education when he developed a video and workshop called F.A.T. City. The workshop simulates the "frustration," "anxiety," and "tension" school experiences pose to students with learning disabilities.

Over the next few pages, I hope you will see many reasons for understanding students at a deeper level. Consider what it would be like to go to a job every day that you knew in advance you could not do. Some students with learning disabilities have this type of experience every day at school. A call to awareness involves an intellectual understanding of students' needs, as well as the emotional sensitivity to realize their ongoing challenge at school.

WHAT'S YOUR POMMEL HORSE?

Being able to tap into the child's point of view is worth the time and effort involved. A great teacher will try to "crawl behind the child's forehead" to assume the perspective of a student. To this end, I would like to share my own perspective of a challenge that I encountered during my school days. In addition, this true story speaks to the following issues:

- The difference between "can't" and "won't," or the existence of a disability as opposed to resistant or avoidant behavior
- The need to adapt tasks to create paths for success and increased self-esteem
- The value of breaking tasks into manageable units that can lead to partial victories and perhaps eventually to total accomplishment

Among my most vivid memories from the all-girls private school I attended, I remember being in gym class, dressed in a light blue tunic with bloomers. A springboard and pommel horse, seemingly 20 feet high, were glaring at me, and the teacher told us, one by one, to run; spring off the board; lean forward into a leap; and simultaneously grab the handlebars of the pommel horse, raise and bend our legs into a crouch position, swish smoothly through the handlebars, and land cleanly on the other side of the horse.

Was she joking?

In 5 years, I never did it. I learned a few things, though:

1. I was never going to succeed at this task.

2. Lucy + pommel horse = fear, bruises, and humiliation.

3. I'd rather get a few laughs than continue the exercise in fear and humiliation. I adjusted the task. I ran, turned aside from the springboard, and ducked under the pommel horse! I picked scolding over humiliation.

What's My Point Here?

What if the teacher had taken the time to adjust the task for me? For example, what if she had instructed me to focus on running, landing squarely and strongly on the center of the springboard, and maintaining my balance while landing on the floor?

What if she had offered choices for me and the number of other students who were not athletically inclined? There is certainly more than one path to skill development and more than one timeline for skill mastery.

What if, as mentioned in the introduction, the teacher had spoken with me directly? She likely would have understood my struggle more completely. We might have been able to exchange views and come up with a plan for success.

What's your "pommel horse"? If you can identify it, you will be able to relate to students who experience difficulties. You will better understand their feelings and connect with them in a way that will lead to an enhanced learning experience for you and them.

THE TOP 10 REASONS TO UNDERSTAND STUDENTS WITH DISABILITIES

Many tasks compete for a teacher's time and attention. Some teachers might feel burdened by the demands placed on them by students with learning disabilities, yet there are compelling reasons to understand such students. Good teachers frequently offer a rationale for a unit of learning; here, the rationale for understanding students with learning disabilities is multifaceted:

1. Most children/adolescents/adults with learning disabilities possess gifts in other areas; understanding goes a long way toward preserving their enthusiasm and energy for continued excellence in their areas of giftedness. Many of these students are athletes, actors, musicians, and/or artists.

2. If your own child had a disability, you would want teachers to understand him, quirks and all.

3. You have learning specialists and psychologists to help you.

4. It is important in terms of human contributions, and it is interesting.

5. Parents will understandably bristle at remarks that insist on correcting a genuine disability.

6. There are legal reasons to do so, including such regulations as the Americans with Disabilities Act, Section 504, and the Individuals with Disabilities Education Act.

7. This is not just for a school. It's for the real world, too. Policies and laws protect the rights of disabled individuals in the workplace.

8. The child did not choose to have the disability.

9. This is an issue of educational diversity. Let's try to understand one another and celebrate our differences.

10. Teachers who understand can develop a child's sense of self-worth.

THE BASE OF THE LEARNING PYRAMID

Visualize the base of a pyramid. In education, this represents attention. A student's attention might wander for a number of reasons:

1. He might be thinking about something else. Called internal distracters, these thoughts may include worries, trying to remember where something is, and so forth.

2. He might be tired. Perhaps he has a long bus ride or sleep problems or his family works long hours. Perhaps he has to attend a sibling's extracurricular practices or games.

3. He might be preoccupied with sounds in the environment. Called external distracters, these sounds may include noises from lawn mowers, students playing outside, and so forth.

4. He might have an organic problem with sustained focus, such as ADHD.

5. He might be depressed and therefore unable to concentrate for regular periods.

6. He might have difficulty distinguishing between foreground and background, resulting in trouble filtering out irrelevant stimuli.

Other conditions can mimic problems with attention. The history and degree of attention-span variability are important considerations for a diagnosis of ADHD. A psychologist experienced in testing and diagnosis is the best resource for probing attention difficulties and making recommendations regarding treatment. This is critical because, unless the base of the pyramid is intact, the student won't "get it" in the first place; then, he will have a hard time responding to it, recalling it, deriving meaning from it, applying it, and so forth. If variable attention exists and is managed, the student will be able to move up the pyramid.

AIR CONDITIONERS AND ANXIETY

For some students, the value of accommodations is tremendous. A teacher's awareness of this value is important in implementing accommodations. I have noticed that when anxious students realize they can have accommodations to help manage their anxiety (e.g., extended time and/or private setting on tests), some of them don't seem to need the accommodations as much. It's as if they benefit from knowing an alternative is available. Simply stated, it's a relief to know there's relief.

I love air conditioners. Aside from the reality that they can make the indoors comfortable on a steamy August day, just knowing that I can manage the heat with the simple twist of a dial seems to keep me cooler.

UNDERKNOWLEDGE

Underknowledge refers to a basic fund of information accumulated over time. It is the result of life experience and formal education. Some students have underknowledge that seems like Swiss cheese—it contains random holes. Others have underknowledge as massive as Fort Knox. I would exercise caution about expectations for underknowledge for the following groups:

- Those new to a school
- Those from a different culture
- Those who have changed schools several times
- Those with specific disabilities (especially those with language-based disabilities, which can spin off socially)

Despite being a vast unknown, underknowledge is often expected to be the same for all students. This is not so. When teachers, coaches, or parents say, "You should know this by now," likely they're referring to recently taught concepts or the murky land of underknowledge.

Developmental issues also come into play when considering underknowledge. Brain research shows that the capacity to think abstractly is not fully developed until about 20 years of age.

DIFFERENT STROKES

Kevin, an 8-year-old, could not remember how to make a capital *I* in cursive, probably because this letter starts with a clockwise motion, which is very different from most other cursive letters (except capital *J*). After tracing in sand, using flocked wallpaper, making Play-Doh letters, and driving little trucks along the road of cursive capital *I*, it was time to adjust my thinking. Kevin could not learn this letter in the "standard" way. I instructed him to make a tiny c and connect it to a wide, lowercase cursive *1*. He got this right away. The process was altered, but the product was fine. Teachers must be ready to alter approaches. Expecting students to learn the same way and achieve mastery at the same time is simply unreasonable. I encourage teachers to step outside the curriculum guide and use their own creativity to offer new approaches and solve problems on an individual basis.

Angela, a 9-year-old, had pronounced dyslexia. One of the most effective approaches to reading instruction is the Orton-Gillingham approach, which is how I began. One day, I flashed the salmon-colored card with the vowel combination AW on it. Instead of responding "A-W says 'aw' as in *saw*," Angela said, "A-W says [long pause] 'uh' [*schwa* sound] as in *was*." I was stunned. She had mastered the technique of associating letter combinations with key words and extracting sounds, but she had processed the letters in reverse. In her mind, she had reversed *saw* as *was*. I used the kinesthetic intensive Fernald technique instead of the favored Orton-Gillingham. Learning is not one-size-fits-all. Be ready to shift gears or even replace the gearbox!

WHEN ROOT WORDS DON'T HELP

English is a difficult language to master. For many students with learning disabilities, even though English is their native language, it can seem more like a foreign language.

It is easy to assume that information is clear; however, it may be necessary to "crawl behind a student's eyebrows" to obtain his perspective. When a student seems confused, ask him to underline the word/words that he finds confusing. Pinpointing language elements can lead to a better understanding of where the breakdown occurs. Words with multiple meanings often pose a challenge to students with learning disabilities. For example, the words *even* and *evenly* may have a similar linguistic structure, but they bring different meanings to various contexts. Compare "Is 34 an even number?" with "Does 7 go into 34 evenly?"

EXPONENTIALLY CONFUSING

If a student has pronounced difficulty interpreting printed symbols, even seemingly simple tasks can prove daunting. Difficulties with spatial perception can cause significant confusion, particularly in math.

Consider the following: x for multiplication is easily confused with x as a designation for a variable. Many math teachers substitute a dot for the x to limit confusion. This helps, and fortunately, the dot is placed above the line on notebook paper so it will not be confused with a decimal or even punctuation, such as part of a colon or semicolon.

Exponents are written above and to the right of a base number; however, negative signs are jotted to the left of the exponent. Sometimes, negative signs are placed between numbers to indicate subtraction. Other times, the minus sign by a number might be floating a bit closer to the line than one used to indicate a negative number. At first glance, a teacher might think the student is confusing math concepts, but it is possible that he is experiencing difficulties related to spatial aware-ness. Knowing, recognizing, and applying "left and right" and "up and down" is not an automatic or reliable process for some students with learning disabilities.

To complicate matters further, different books and teachers jot expressions in their own way. For example, the first letter of the alphabet can appear as A and/or a. If a 1 and 3 are placed close together, the result may look like a B instead of 13. The letter *t* can look a lot like a + unless it's carefully formed. Handwriting and the choice of font can affect a student's understanding and performance at school. Generally, the ability to attend to fine visual details is referred to as visual discrimination. Many students with learning disabilities have specific trouble with visual discrimination.

Teachers can perform a task analysis to see the various steps involved. Many tasks that appear simple (e.g., copying) actually involve complex perceptual interpretation and replication of visual sequences and spatial relations.

A strategy for managing this type of task is to "think out loud." Adding language and auditory feedback can help students comprehend the nature of printed symbols. Try "reading" this equation out loud:

$$6x - 9^{-6} + -3x - 0.5 = t \qquad \text{Solve for t when } x = +9.$$

Imagine you are dyslexic or tired, spilled water on the page, got the last copy before the ink ran out, or can't find your glasses. If you can imagine these scenarios, you are closer to developing the sensitivity needed to understand students with learning disabilities.

BRIDGE FREEZES

I read this road sign a thousand times. Bridge Freezes Before Road Surface. I couldn't understand what it meant. I don't usually have a comprehension problem, but this sign was totally out of context. It made no sense. What did *before* mean? I analyzed the phrase. In my mind, since I noticed the words *surface* and *road*, I related the word *before* to the lateral surface of the pavement. This would mean that the area just in front of the junction of the road and bridge would freeze before the actual bridge span. This made absolutely no sense to me. It was years before I realized that the word *before* was relating to a temporal concept rather than a spatial concept.

Once again, "crawl behind a student's eyebrows" to obtain her perspective. If a student doesn't comprehend a phrase, ask her to underline the confusing word/words. I would have pinpointed *before* as the word that stymied me. Once again, words with multiple meanings often pose a challenge. Be cautious about their use, particularly in high-risk situations (tests, road signs, etc.).

GAIL WELLIN'S HANDWRITING

Spending a few moments to tap into the child's point of view is valuable. To this end, I share a story from my own school experience that speaks to the issue of diversity. Educational diversity is worthy of formal consideration. Some students may have perfect handwriting, and others may exhibit other strengths. The mix of students enriches the entire environment.

I remember it from the first grade. It was perfect. It was everything my handwriting was not. I envied it. I tried to emulate it. I really tried.

I developed a huge callus on my middle finger from holding the pencil with a death grip. My handwriting did not come close to looking like Gail Wellin's. Years later, I realized that Gail Wellin's pencil had soft lead!

What do you recall from your childhood at school? Reflecting on personal experiences can link a teacher's past to a student's present. The ability to perceive an experience from another's perspective is to be valued as the art and heart of teaching.

SUMMARY

Once an evaluation is completed, the reasons for a student's difficulties with academic, behavioral, or emotional issues are revealed. The teachers can then have an intellectual understanding of what will be needed to help the student. Subsequently, they can establish a plan and take actions to provide the best possible educational program for that student. Over the years, they can share the explanation and will be enlightened about the student's needs. This is, however, only part of what it will take to connect to the student in a meaningful way.

Developing sensitivity for the challenges faced by learning-disabled students is essential. The effect disabilities have on a child's learning and self-esteem is real and ongoing. Depending on the age of the student, multiple hurdles, obstacles, and difficulties will have been a considerable part of the child's school experience to this point. Connecting to the problems faced by the student will require cultivating empathy.

Once teachers, parents, and others have identified their own "pommel horse," they will have a greater ability to tap into how facing a difficulty feels. This empathy will allow them to develop a much closer connection with the student.

2 Student Needs

Clarifying and Understanding

Throughout the school year, a teacher learns about a student through his performance on homework assignments, projects, classroom evaluations, standardized tests, and classroom participation. But grades do not tell the whole story. The teacher gains information about far more than just content mastery. A student's mastery of skills vital to future learning is constantly being studied. How does the child fare with reading comprehension, listening comprehension, writing, speaking, and mathematical thinking and computation? Moving beyond foundational skills, the teacher learns about a child's work pace, organizational skills, intellectual curiosity, comfort at school, memory, verbal expression, social skills, ability to sustain attention, creativity, and even mood.

How does the question of learning disabilities arise? Perhaps a child is noted to speak knowledgeably, but her knowledge gets lost on written work; a young man exhibits fluent reading but cannot recall or derive meaning from what he has read; or a hardworking fifth grader demonstrates strong organizational skills and exemplary effort, but her test performance is disappointing. When there is a pattern of inconsistencies and discrepancies, as in the examples noted above, one cannot help but wonder why, and asking if the student has learning disabilities is appropriate.

Responding to these inconsistencies involves both interventions and evaluation to address the problem and know the cause. If support is readily available, that can be the first step. Many of the strategies listed in Chapter 6 can be implemented without delay. These strategies can help a great deal. In most school settings, however, interventions that involve accommodation can only be implemented with documentation of need. This will require obtaining an evaluation by an accredited specialist. In the world of medicine, when a child visits the pediatrician due to a problematic cough, the physician can treat the symptom with medicine; however, the underlying cause of the cough is often examined through testing. Interventions can address the need, and evaluations can promote understanding.

A learning specialist is trained to recognize symptoms of various learning disorders. Also, as noted at the back of this book, there are excellent online resources that can help others learn about various conditions. As most learning disabilities are lifelong conditions, both parents and students will benefit tremendously from becoming experts on the condition.

Evaluations identify strengths and needs. It is often the case that a student with learning disabilities possesses remarkable gifts. Educational theorist, acclaimed author, and professor Howard Gardner (1983) disputed long-standing ideas about intelligence. Rather, he identified eight distinct intelligences: linguistic, logical-mathematical, spatial, bodily-kinesthetic, musical, interpersonal, intrapersonal, and naturalist. At school, this theory is evident in many combinations of needs and gifts, such as dyslexic students who excel in math, dysgraphic students who are gifted musicians, and memory-challenged students who are celebrated athletes.

It is often said that knowledge is power. Self-knowledge will be tremendously empowering for a student with learning disabilities. Demystification refers to the process of guiding a student to learn as much as possible about her own strengths and needs. The examiner who conducted the evaluation is in the best position to provide demystification. Once a clear understanding of issues has been achieved, students can be respectfully involved in solutions designed to address their needs.

SEVEN GOOD REASONS

I don't want to jump the gun and recommend an evaluation if simple support can improve a child's performance. On the other hand, in some situations, a psychoeducational evaluation would be appropriate and valuable. Consider the following factors:

1. Greater understanding of issues is desired.

    The variety or intensity of concerns warrants the services of a psychologist.

2. Documentation is required for accommodations and special services.

    Many educational institutions (e.g., SAT, colleges) require documentation before they provide extended time on testing. In general, if used for this reason, an evaluation is good for 3 years and will need to be updated beyond that time.

3. The school and the parents view the child very differently.

   Individual administration and interpretation of standardized tests by an outside specialist may help provide an objective perspective.

4. A conscientious student is doing poorly.

   What (if anything) could the school do to help? Are the expectations reasonable?

5. Supportive services have been tried without appreciable benefit.

   Is the child getting the right kind and/or the right amount of help?

6. Retention or an alternative placement is being considered.

   The opinion of an outside specialist can be helpful. Counseling tools like the Light's Retention Scale can also be administered at this time.

7. A student has attended many schools within a short period.

   Because different schools have different grading systems and curricula, it may be valuable to have standardized information about achievement and potential.

SOFT SIGNS OF DYSGRAPHIA

Dysgraphia is a disorder of written expression. In my experience, the number of students with dysgraphia has been increasing steadily over the past 10 years. Students with this difficulty have trouble getting their thoughts on paper. This manifests with mechanical difficulties (handwriting, spelling, punctuation, etc.), processing speed (slow to get ideas out), or development of ideas. The diagnosis is made according to the type and frequency of errors as compared with other students of the same age. Looking at writing samples can be very telling. The learning specialist can study journal entries and get quite a bit of informal information. Naturally, many of the difficulties listed below will be common for younger students. It is important to keep developmental issues in mind, but here are some specifics:

- *Q* or *Y* has tail going the wrong way.
- 5 or 3 is reversed.
- *U* or *W* has mini tail (last stroke) on wrong side of letter.
- Student has trouble with sequencing—for example, he writes "thier" for *their* or "frist" for *first*.
- Words run together with little space in between.
- Words float above the line, drag below the line, and/or split the line.

- Multiple self-corrections are evident in erasures and strikethroughs.
- Spelling errors occur on grade-appropriate words.
- Letters show a random mix of capital and lowercase.
- Writing shows a mix of cursive and manuscript.
- Slant is inconsistent, so letters tilt in opposite directions.
- Size of writing is inappropriate, often too large for age and grade.
- Lines drawn freehand (e.g., for columns) appear wobbly.

Teachers often remark that a dysgraphic student demonstrates strong verbal skills in class participation. The discrepancy between oral and written skills can be pronounced.

DEGREES OF DIFFERENCE

Educators have made great strides in noting and reporting "high risk" signs, such as reversals, restlessness, distractibility, impulsivity, extended response time, discrepancy between spoken and written skills, and so forth. Since many students exhibit one or all of these signs from time to time, it is important to bear in mind the effect of the difficulties:

- Is this behavior interfering with the student's performance at school? To what degree?
- Is this behavior interfering with other students' performance at school? To what degree?
- Are there strategies and accommodations that could improve the student's behavior and performance?
- Are these supports "reasonable" to implement? Is the amount of time, the effort, the number of trained personnel required, and the cost reasonable?
- Will the student accept the support? Will he receive help willingly and not shy away from suggestions and feedback?

CAN'T VERSUS WON'T

"Can't versus won't" is the same as "disability versus refusal and/or avoidance." The difference can be hard to discern; however, a full psychoeducational evaluation can clarify the distinction. Sometimes, a student with a pronounced disability will avoid a certain task, in large part because it is extremely difficult. In a situation like that, there is a distinct "can't," as well as a bit of "won't." Procrastination or avoidance is a natural reaction to an extremely challenging task. When a student is not performing as expected, distinguishing a "can't" from a "won't" can help educators and parents solve problems. What is needed? Perhaps offering one-on-one instruction, as well as accommodations, will be the best response to a "can't." Providing a motivational system could be the best response for a short-term "won't."

SIX BOX

The "Six Box" is a structured form of note taking that helps with educational review and planning. I use it in most meetings, to prepare for parent conferences, and to review a child's records.

I made a sample and jotted some notes to give an idea of what can be put in the boxes. The "Six Box" is one of my favorite educational tools. I use it frequently. See a sample "Six Box" at the end of this chapter.

DIG IN!

Now is the time to look to resources (see the end of the book), such as wonderful Web sites (e.g., LDonline.org) or helpful magazines (e.g., *ADDitude*), and learn. Knowledge of terminology, including terms that reference aspects of a disability, as well as those that relate to educational planning, will be important. Ask questions. Consider joining a support group. Find a mentor if possible. None of us came into the world with a guidebook for children, and this is particularly true for parents of children with disabilities. In the end, you and the child must be the ultimate experts about the condition affecting the child's education.

SUMMARY

The learning specialist's observation of the soft signs of a disorder can prompt discussion of an evaluation. Other reasons to consider evaluation include the "Seven Good Reasons" noted in this chapter. Regardless of whether an evaluation is completed, an analysis of student performance will be valuable in reviewing the educational program of any child who struggles at school. In this regard, a "Six Box" can represent a clear and logical summary of past, present, and future issues that have directed, are directing, and can continue to direct the student's educational program. For conferences, when sharing information about the student, an instrument, such as the "Six Box," will clarify key elements to be considered and acted upon.

Example of Six Box		
Strong	***Average***	***Difficulties***
List areas that are above average according to grades and standardized testing: Academics Effort Social Emotional Arts Athletics Interests outside of school *The strengths may offer insight about the best ways to address areas of need.*	*List areas that are generally OK.*	*List academic troubles. Jot challenges the child has encountered:* Parents' divorce Medical issues *List other miscellaneous information:* 4 schools in 5 years Long commute to school Intense sibling rivalry
Tried	***Needs***	***Questions***
List interventions: Parent conferences Written communication to family Extended time on tests (2x) Outside evaluation *(put date)* Medication Retention Consultation with psychologist Consultation with learning specialist Vision tested Summer work Tutoring 2x a week in Grade 3 Assistive technology Counseling/therapy in Grade 4 Preferential seating in class Teachers signing homework book *I mark successful interventions with a +, and then I include them in the NEEDS column to the right.*	*List interventions that have already been tried and were successful. List new ideas, including supports and accommodation, that you have not tried.*	*Jot any issues that do not seem to "fit" with the picture:* Why are these problems presenting now? What is a typical school night like for the child at home? What is a child's preferred learning style? Is the child happy? Where does the child complete homework?

3 Parents

Informing and Supporting

There are a number of viewpoints to be carefully considered within the educational program of any student with learning disabilities. The teacher's perspective is well known to most readers. The student's viewpoint is clear through the information provided by an assessment, as well as conferences and conversations that have taken place over the years. The parents' perspective is critical to forging a strong partnership between home and school; however, it is often not fully understood.

To establish a constructive and positive connection, it is key to establish open communication. Teachers, examiners, and administrators have much to convey about a student's performance. Often, however, the parents will perceive their child in a different way. When meeting with parents, allow plenty of time for their response. It is possible to learn about both the child and the parents' acceptance of difficulties.

As mentioned earlier, acceptance will have a strong impact on the delivery and value of support services. In fact, like the student, the parents must travel the road of awareness, acceptance, and advocacy. In the *Journal of Learning Disabilities*, Lynn Stoll Switzer (1985) wrote about her work with parents. After working to increase their understanding of learning disabilities, the majority of parents showed decreased anxiety and greater acceptance of the diagnosis.

Parents often need to coordinate outside support, including tutors and counselors. This may be a whole new world to them. Teachers can help enormously by guiding them through the selection process. Parent approval enables teachers and outside specialists to coordinate efforts through open communication, so this connection must be established early on.

Parents new to the world of learning disabilities may find themselves overwhelmed with the process, the terminology, and particularly the emotions that accompany this new journey. Teachers can direct parents to resources that will help the entire family adjust. Many such resources are noted at the end of this book.

LIMITS TO CONFERENCE

If teachers anticipate scheduling a parent conference to discuss a child's special needs, it is important to understand the parents' trouble with hearing such a message. Understanding the emotional component in awareness and acceptance will be a key factor in your delivery. Parents need to know how the difficulties play out in school, to what extent they impact learning, and how often they are evident. Most importantly, parents need to know what can be done to help. This is a lot for anyone to hear, so this type of meeting cannot be rushed. Allow at least 50 minutes to cover the important points and expect responses. Often, it's not possible for teachers to be present for the entire conference, so collect input in advance for those who cannot attend or can only stay for a short time. It's not necessary to have an army of people at this meeting. Parents could feel outnumbered and get defensive. As expected, the complete picture will include sharing the student's strengths. This meeting will challenge communication skills, receptivity, and trust. Focus on sharing the top-priority needs. The parents may well feel overwhelmed even with that information. In public schools, procedures, timelines, rights, and resources will be explained. As a courtesy, exchange e-mail information so parents can follow up with questions or concerns once they have had an opportunity to digest the information.

COMMUNICATING SENSITIVELY AND ACCURATELY

Sometimes, it's necessary to qualify the degree of a disability. Adjectives like *mild* and *moderate* are easy to apply. More serious disabilities can be tricky to communicate accurately and sensitively. My favorite term in such cases is *pronounced*. For example,

> Gulliver has "pronounced" processing-speed issues.
>
> Jennifer exhibits "pronounced" organizational difficulties.

TEACHERS AS PARENTS

If you are a teacher as well as a parent, you may recall school conferences where you were on the receiving end of the information. Recollections of personal experiences can guide you toward knowing effective strategies for communication. By establishing a desire to understand the student more fully, parents and teachers share a common goal and can form a partnership.

WHO SAID WHAT?

When a parent-teacher conference involves laying the groundwork for any type of intervention (evaluation, special support, retention), note taking is important. Being able to reference different viewpoints expressed could be valuable after the conference. If all teachers take notes, it's a bit intimidating for parents. Assign one person to take notes during the conference. This way, teachers can establish eye contact with the parents.

PRECONFERENCE PREPARATION

Using a graphic tool like the "Six Box" (see Chapter 2) will help participants in a conference present information in an organized manner. Explain the following:

- What difficulties does the child exhibit?
- What strategies/support have been tried to meet the child's needs?
- What strengths does the child demonstrate?
- What do you recommend to address the child's needs more fully?
- Finally, ask any questions that seem pertinent. Does the child seem happy at school? What happens after school?

DOESN'T WANT TO BE DIFFERENT

I've been in numerous meetings where a parent submits an evaluation that substantiates a student's need for accommodations and support. Paying special attention to the recommendations, I explain what the school is able to do and what responsibilities the student, the family, and outside support persons might assume as well. At this point, sometimes a parent expresses hesitation, saying, "My child doesn't want to appear different." I acknowledge this predicament, as well as a child's strong desire to fit in with his or her peers; however, this scenario is impossible to manage. To access support and accommodations that are distinct from the regular program, the student will need to be onboard. I review the three As: awareness, acceptance, and advocacy. I tell the parent a few times that I hope the child will meet me halfway and that the compromise will prove to be worth the temporary discomfort. I guide the parent to "let the tape run a bit" to see how things play out. Perhaps, if the child sees that other students are willing to accept support, this discovery will tip the scale.

TUTOR'S CHALLENGE

If a tutor is good, she will work on a skill that is challenging for the student. This is important to remember in assessing student attitudes and responses to tutoring in the beginning sessions.

To maintain a good relationship, the tutor will need to find ways to make the task enjoyable, as well as provide breaks and check in with the student about his interests. It's not uncommon for children to complain about tutoring, particularly in the initial weeks. I suggest parents use the "Five Try" technique. By then, the student and tutor will have established a rapport, and the student will see that the tutoring is effective.

If the student complains after five lessons, it's possible that the "chemistry" is not working between the tutor and the student. Several elements may be coming into play in such a situation: The student may need a different tutor, or the scheduled time for the lesson may be undesirable (Fridays and evenings are not popular). The biggest obstacle occurs if the student has not reached a point where he can accept help—that is, if he has not achieved acceptance of his limitations and needs. Acceptance is something that occurs at different times for individual students. Rarely can a tutor hasten the process of acceptance.

THE INVISIBLE DISABILITIES

Much has been written on this topic. I exaggerate here to bring home a point. I do not in any way mean to be insensitive to people with handicaps or disabilities. They are my heroes. If a person has a cleft palate, does it help to bring this to his or her attention? Surely that person is well aware of the condition. What about the parents' attention? Don't they already know about it? Should the person be penalized for the condition? Raise the same questions for persons with hearing impairment, verbal dysfluency (stammering, stuttering), artificial limbs, and so forth. It's ridiculous and harsh, isn't it? I imagine someone removing my spectacles and insisting that I try to look more closely. Persons with dysgraphia, dyslexia, anxiety, ADHD, executive dysfunction, short-term memory problems, and so forth may not be easy to identify. Learning disabilities have been called the invisible disabilities. Persons with these disabilities have little to no control over their condition(s). Naturally, it does not help to caution them to pay attention, read more carefully, and so forth. Providing support, strategies, and accommodations is the way to go.

CRAFTING REPORTS ON STUDENTS WITH NEEDS

Before writing a comment, it's important for teachers to see if the student has a documented disability. Having this information on hand can help in crafting accurate and sensitive comments on areas of need.

The following is an example of a brief teacher comment on a student with documented ADHD who continues to require support:

> I understand that Jessica needs to be seated up front, and I am pleased to see her respond positively to redirects and cueing. She also benefits substantially from using the AlphaSmart to take notes. I have noticed that her focus has been more variable recently than earlier in the year. I will speak with her privately about other strategies I might use to help manage her distractibility.

THE VALUE OF EVALUATION

I presented the case for an evaluation to a rather gun-shy mother. I explained that the school develops a Student Learning Plan, often referred to as an Individualized Educational Plan, or IEP, to summarize the evaluation's finding. Within the plan, documented strengths and needs are listed. The evaluation and plan promote a comprehensive awareness of strategies, supports, and accommodations that can be incorporated into the child's educational program. The mother asked about the stigma and "labeling" she associated with testing and supportive services.

I explained that those who are diagnosed with disabilities are now legally empowered. I cited the cancellation of the practice of "flagging" on standardized tests (SATs, etc.) and the climate of acceptance in institutions of higher learning. I went on to say that I believe allowing needs to remain unrecognized is a much greater risk than recognizing and managing needs.

VERY BRIGHT?

In an attempt to provide reassurance and hope to families, educators sometimes characterize a child as "very bright" when in fact he or she is "average" in ability. There is nothing wrong with being "average," but it is not the same as being "very bright." Parents may not be familiar with the terminology related to intelligence quotients, but they probably assume that "very bright" means really smart. Understandably, they have high hopes. When I'm describing a student of average intellect, I say he or she has "solid" capabilities and demonstrates potential within the average range.

DESCRIBING HYPERACTIVITY

In class, students may exhibit many behaviors that are typical of people with hyperactivity disorder. When speaking with parents to describe behaviors, use verbs as opposed to adjectives. Naming the behavior helps families see and hear specifically what is happening and seems less judgmental than using adjectives. When first learning to document behavior, I had to invent new terms to describe what I had seen. Develop some expressions to convey specific behaviors. Here are my observations about one hyperactive student's behaviors, along with the degree to which they were presented:

- Strokes hair—constant (virtually incessant for 40 minutes)
- Drums fingers on tabletop—intermittent
- Jiggles right leg—constant
- Swings leg—intermittent
- Chews cheek—briefly
- Wrinkles nose—infrequently
- Talks fast—routinely
- Wraps arm around back of head and covers ear with cupped hand (possibly to filter noise?)
- Puckers mouth and sucks
- Nibbles fingers—often
- Calls out in loud voice (three times)

I shared with parents my perception of the degree to which these behaviors interfered with the student's, as well as the class's, learning and comfort. Looking at the list of behaviors above, it seems that this student would be totally exhausted at the end of 40 minutes. Actually, he was an engaged learner, made positive contributions to the class, and smiled frequently.

SUMMARY

When school and parents confer about students with special needs, the skill and art of communication figure largely into the success of meetings. Teachers' careful descriptions of in-class observations can help parents visualize their child in an environment worlds apart from that at home. As the "Describing Hyperactivity" section emphasizes, the use of verbs as opposed to adjectives tells what the child does. This comes across without the judgment that can be inferred with the use of adjectives.

Consider how a parent might react to hearing "Your child rocks in his seat, fidgets with items on the desktop, and swings his legs throughout class." Now, consider if this same scenario had been communicated as "Your child is hyperactive." The parent's reaction to these two different remarks could be significantly disparate and quite possibly affect the outcome and tone of a conference.

Parents and educators must make concerted efforts to remain sensitive, respectful, and open to hearing the different ways a child presents. These efforts will build trust. Naturally, the recommendation for an evaluation may cause the family some anxiety; however, if prior communications with the school have been accurate and clear, it is probable that such a recommendation will ultimately be accepted. Once an evaluation is completed, it is crucial that teachers remain aware of the findings in the report. Trust can be easily violated if educators report the shortcomings of a child after a disability has been documented and accommodations and supports have been recommended. Imagine a family's reaction to following the school's suggestion to obtain an evaluation, submitting the report, and later receiving a communication that focuses on the child's known disability. Written reports need to be crafted with care. Meetings will be the most productive when communications are sensitive and clear and the attitude of participants remains open, respectful, and trusting.

4 The Program

Facilitation, Support, and Consultation

Over the years, many people have asked me about the program for students with learning disabilities. Parents and students alike are not always clear about who can receive help from the learning specialist. The answer depends largely on the school (public or private) and also reflects the level of acceptance of the administration, teachers, students, and parents.

Ideally, a learning specialist should be able to work with any student who needs help. This is called direct service. The learning specialist teaches the student. Aside from meeting public school eligibility requirements, finding time for direct service is often the most difficult challenge. The student's schedule is a factor in determining how often and when he can meet with the learning specialist. Sometimes, the results of an evaluation indicate a learning disability, such as dyslexia, with underpinnings in phonological difficulties. When this occurs, the school may find it appropriate to defer study of a foreign language. In this case, the student can meet with the learning specialist during foreign language time. Another possible time for direct service is during study hall. While direct service may benefit a student to a great extent, it may not be possible during the school day. When this happens, the learning specialist will often recommend outside tutoring. Within the public sector, there are clear guidelines about justification for direct service, how much support is appropriate, who will provide such support, and how and when progress will be evaluated.

Besides providing direct service to students, a learning specialist facilitates accommodations. If an evaluation documents the need for extended time on testing, the student usually takes her test in the learning specialist's room. Similarly, if a reader or scribe is needed for work or assessments, the learning specialist would read or write for the student. In fact, the learning specialist facilitates the implementation of any reasonable accommodation.

Another key function of the learning specialist is consultation. Particularly at the high school level, faculty members are experts in their respective content areas, but they may not be as well versed in learning differences or developmental issues. The learning specialist can support teachers by examining files or providing in-class observations. Such clues as a pattern of behavior or performance or a long-standing history of similar comments may lead to suggestions about ways to manage the difficulties; they may also confirm the degree of difficulty teachers perceive. The consultation piece can be very valuable in helping establish an educational plan that will yield more success. For example, simply assigning a seat in the place closest to the teacher can reduce the field of distraction and provide easy redirects or cueing for attention. This leads to more on-task behavior for a student with variable attention. The provision of a portable writing instrument (laptop or AlphaSmart) can help another student manage writing assignments without difficulty.

The program of support provided by the learning specialist encompasses direct service, facilitation of accommodations, and consultation with other educators. As a result, teachers will see the learning specialist teaching students (one-on-one and occasionally in groups), reading or scribing for students, and sitting in classes to observe student performance and behavior.

THE THREE *A*s OF MEETING LEARNING NEEDS

Awareness

Establishing a successful plan begins with an awareness of the student's needs. This can be a difficult step for some families and students to take. Several components can facilitate awareness:

- School history, including past teacher remarks and grades
- Teacher feedback about current performance
- Parent perspectives and history
- Results of standardized group testing

The key feature for developing a comprehensive awareness of learning needs, however, comes in the form of an evaluation. The evaluation needs to be current, with the general rule of thumb being 3 years old or fewer. Once testing is complete, the examiner (usually a psychologist) interprets results for families, educators, and the student. This step is essential in developing an understanding. If other specialists (tutors, counselors, physicians) are involved, the information should be shared with them as well.

Acceptance

This step is a bit more complicated and much less predictable. Students must accept that their learning needs are substantially different from others'. Students come to acceptance at different times. I support the "Five Try" model, and encourage students to try a new strategy, accommodation, or support five times. After five tries, students usually perceive the value of the support and are accepting. A school climate of acceptance can facilitate a student's acceptance. In the end, the student needs to come to terms with her own learning needs.

Advocacy

This is something of an art. Adults are generally advocates for younger children whose language and interpersonal skills are still developing. In a middle school, advisors often advocate for their advisees. As students mature, however, they can and should begin to advocate for themselves. Students who operate at this level have moved from accepting differences to asking for help managing them. They realize that teachers may occasionally need a reminder. They are comfortable with their own unique needs and self-confident in their abilities to negotiate for themselves. To my mind, they are courageous, independent, persistent, and positive. Learning specialists can role-play with students or develop scripts to encourage appropriate self-advocacy among students.

TALKING WITH STUDENTS ABOUT LEARNING PLANS

Students need to know what to expect from teachers, as well as what teachers will expect from them. This will involve one-on-one communication. The parent, advisor, or learning specialist may assume that responsibility.

I emphasize the positive. For example, I might say any of the following to the student:

- "We have ways to help you do your best at school, including letting you have extra time on tests."
- "There are steps you can take to improve your own learning, including sitting in the front row, collecting Penned Notes [see Chapter 5] after class, and using an AlphaSmart for in-class journal entries."

- "Feel free to remind teachers about your need for extra time on tests."
- I like to emphasize the team aspect of the plan and often say, "If you do your part and we do our part, I think your learning and experience at school will be much improved."

In my opinion, explaining the results of testing (including diagnoses) should be left to the professionals, such as the examiner who prepared the report. This process, referred to as demystification, can be especially valuable for older students.

WHO GOES THERE?

Thinking hypothetically, what if, at some point, every student was directed to take a test in the learning specialist's room? This action has the potential to do several things:

- Familiarize each student with the room and the learning specialist
- Increase comfort level with the support system
- Continue to de-stigmatize the program
- Offer every child opportunities to learn one-on-one strategies
- Give the learning specialist an opportunity to observe test-taking behavior

With the above goals in mind, I allow students who do not have formally documented needs come to my room for support during study halls. This arrangement may not be possible in every school, but there are numerous benefits, as stated above.

LEARNING SPECIALISTS ARE LIKE ACUPUNCTURISTS

Learning specialists are like acupuncturists without the needles. The main focus is treatment. Diagnosis is informal and related to problem solving. Learning specialists in private schools can operate outside a rigid system. The system is dissimilar to an HMO. Students don't need a formal referral for a learning specialist. A student might get scheduled faster if she is "pre-approved," but supportive services are available to any student. On any given day, I see "non-approved" students who ask for help studying for a test or editing a paper. Naturally, providing accommodations is quite different from offering support. Ongoing accommodation can be provided only with formal documentation of need.

BETTER THAN GOING THE EXTRA MILE

Better than going the extra mile is seeking a different route. I place a high value on a student's willingness to try something different and/or approach it differently; to experiment with options; to seek alternate solutions; and to inquire about possibilities and travel new roads to arrive at the destination. For a student with learning disabilities, those around him who cultivate acceptance and value difference will greatly improve his sense of self-worth.

NOT JUST FOR STUDENTS WITH DISABILITIES

My priority is to work with students who have documented disabilities. I facilitate accommodations, provide direct support, and act as a liaison with faculty and families. Still, students without disabilities come to my room, either by teacher recommendation or self-referral. This keeps other students guessing as to exactly who sees me. It gives fluidity to the program and minimizes stigma. Unlike public school systems where qualifying for services involves a formal procedure, private schools have the luxury of providing a "revolving door" model based on needs that may be long-standing or short term. For example, I recently

- Loaned an AlphaSmart to an eighth grader who wants to improve her note taking in class.
- Provided quiet space to a child recovering from illness who is working to catch up on assignments.
- Acted as a scribe for a student on a math test so the teacher could see all the steps to the problems (called diagnostic prescriptive test taking).
- Worked one-on-one with a student to weed out papers and restore order to a binder in distress.
- Provided storage space and reminders for a new student who struggles to manage his materials and schedule.

  Question: Which of the above cases do you think involves a student with documented learning disabilities?

  Answer: None.

WHEN LESS IS MORE

I am grateful for the phenomenal technology at my school. Many students delight in exploring the capabilities of a computer. This research is great at the appropriate time, but when students need to focus on one task, the Internet can be an undesirable temptation. When students need to focus on writing, I have found the AlphaSmart, which runs on AA batteries and is lightweight and durable, to be a valuable tool. It cannot access the Internet but can check spelling, and written work produced on the AlphaSmart can be downloaded on a computer for further editing if needed and then printed. Another advantage over computers: It automatically saves. A writer needs to make two intentional steps to delete work. Students can use it for in-class journal writing and note taking. Teachers never worry that a student might be on the Internet. The Web site for this tool is listed at the end of this book.

RECORDED BOOKS

As you know, listening to books on tape or CD can improve comprehension and fluency measurably. The combination of the spoken and printed word is powerful. An obvious fit for students with reading disabilities, this can also develop literary appreciation in other students. Some companies offer titles with a choice of two controlled speeds for reading text; one is 17% slower than the other. There's a wide range of offerings from elementary age through higher education. Families of reluctant or disabled readers are likely to be grateful for this information.

If the student has a documented reading disorder (dyslexia), she should be eligible for Recordings for the Blind and Dyslexic, otherwise known as RFB&D. This organization is an excellent resource, and membership cost is reasonable considering the comprehensive support services. Check your local library and the Web (see Resources at the end of this book).

APPLIANCE MANUALS

Have you ever read the manual that accompanies a new appliance? In the back of the manual, it usually says something like "*Before* you call the repairperson, make sure that you have checked to see that the appliance is properly plugged into an outlet, checked to see that the appliance is turned on," and so forth.

The idea is to do a little troubleshooting before you call in the troops. The same idea holds true for students having trouble at school. Many public school systems require teachers to document interventions they have tried before initiating a referral for special services. If the problems are long-standing or pronounced, it's appropriate to implement supportive services right away. If the student is new to a teacher or the school, however, it's a good idea to try different strategies or simple supports before recommending tutoring, an evaluation, or counseling. Simple adjustments or alternative approaches may alleviate the difficulties.

SPLIT-PEA SOUP

People often say a taste can be acquired. The key is to try something new a few times. I'm not sure this is true with everything. Split-pea soup was pretty much a one-taste item for me.

For students, developing a liking for a particular genre or topic may come in time. The same is true for acceptance of accommodations and support. The first time these suggestions are offered, some students will jump right in, but some won't. This is when adults need to encourage the "Five Try" approach. It's not possible to know if a new support will work right away. Tell students they need to try it five times. After five tries, ask questions that reflect the effectiveness of the support. Students may not feel entirely comfortable with the support, but they may have noticed its positive impact on their academics. If they see that the support is effective, they will continue with it, and over time, their comfort with it will increase.

Encourage the "Five-Try" approach but maybe not with split-pea soup or fruitcake.

ACCOMMODATION WITHOUT DOCUMENTATION

A teacher came to me and shared the following interesting set of circumstances. A student seemed distracted during a test and did poorly; her parent complained that the distraction prevented the child from demonstrating knowledge and asked that she be permitted to take tests outside the classroom in a less distracting environment (the learning specialists' room). I made the following points during my response:

1. The frequency and degree of distractibility must be considered. If a child is frequently distracted, attentional abilities may be a genuine consideration; therefore, more formal documentation, such as an evaluation, would be appropriate.

2. Most children test better in a distraction-free environment, so out-of-the-ordinary needs must be evident.

3. "Least restrictive environment" (LRE) is a key phrase in supportive education. The idea behind this concept is to keep the child within a regular program as much as possible, for as long as she can be successful. The idea is minimum intervention. LRE would probably not support having the child take the test in a separate room.

4. Sometimes, the learning specialist can monitor a child's progress on a test to observe if there is a distinct pattern in test taking. This works well in cases where an evaluation is not desirable. This accommodation could be used in an informal diagnostic manner.

5. The reality is that a limited number of spaces are available for test takers in the learning specialist's room. These spaces should be reserved primarily for students with written documentation of need (an evaluation 3 years old or less) and a Student Learning Plan or IEP.

LIFE VEST

Dr. Martha Bridge Denckla is an internationally known researcher and clinician in the area of developmental cognitive neurology. She currently directs the Developmental Cognitive Neurology Clinic at the Kennedy Krieger Institute. At a conference, she used a life vest as an analogy for support systems for students with disabilities. The "nonswimmers" represented students with disabilities. I love Dr. Denckla's explanation and carry it a bit further here:

> A life vest can enable nonswimmers to get around in the water while they develop their swimming skills. Some children practice hard and get great instruction. As a result, they build muscles, skills, and confidence and become swimmers. Voilà—the life vest comes off, and these new swimmers can participate in activities anywhere in the pool. For students with disabilities, sustaining support while developing skills can be tricky. Here are some questions to consider.

> ### Is the nonswimmer willing to wear the vest in a pool where others are not?

If not, skill development can be pretty shaky, and progress will likely be slow. Is the child eager to learn the skills necessary to participate in the activity? He has to want to swim. Motivation is key.

Can the nonswimmer participate in private swimming lessons?

Time and money are usually needed. A good instructor must be identified. The student must be willing to participate. The parents must provide the transportation and allocate the time.

Will the nonswimmer do strengthening exercises at home?

Drills can be tedious but are often necessary to build the muscles needed for the activity. Will a life vest do the trick in all waters? Are there areas where even those with a life vest may not be safe?

Not all waters are safe for nonswimmers. Deep or fast-moving waters and/or waters without steps or a shallow end may not be safe for nonswimmers. The pool may be overcrowded, and if supervision is not adequate, even with a vest, it may not be safe for nonswimmers to enter. What happens when the vest comes off? When can a nonswimmer remove the vest?

It depends. If the swimmer has a permanent or chronic condition resulting in a serious handicap, the vest may need to remain permanently. In other cases, different flotation devices can be substituted for the vest. Nonswimmers can progress from a full vest to arm doughnuts. The degree of the disability is an important issue. Assessment is a key factor in determining the need for support.

SUPPORT PERSONS—WHO DOES WHAT?

Academic Coach

An academic coach works with a student on a *regular* basis to offer support and encouragement on assignments. Students with time management, sustained attention, or perseverance and effort issues often benefit from an academic coach. Generally, an academic coach is needed on a long-term basis since the presenting issues are lifelong. A coach must be encouraging and positive by nature. He must model dependability, punctuality, and organization. Management of assignments and organization are the main goals.

Tutor

A tutor provides direct instruction in a specific content area. Children who struggle with math or upper-level science often benefit from a tutor. There are SAT tutors as well. Some tutors have training in specialized reading techniques, such as the Orton-Gillingham method. Tutoring is skill specific and may be intensive but time limited. Content mastery is the goal.

Learning Specialist

A learning specialist teaches strategies to address global academic issues, such as reading comprehension, writing, test taking, test preparation, and so forth. A learning specialist facilitates accommodations required to address documented learning needs. A degree in learning disabilities is expected for a learning specialist. The duration and intensity of support provided to students varies according to placement and expectations. For example, a gifted dyslexic student in high school may need long-term support since college is probably desirable.

LEVELS OF SUPPORT

When students are referred for help with core academic problems, such as reading and writing, it's a good idea to provide both remediation and classroom support.

Remediation

Remediation is specialized instruction that builds academic skills that are initially below standard.

Support

Support is instruction that provides study strategies using topics and materials that are concurrently used in the student's classroom.

I worked with a student who has reading, spelling, and memory problems. We studied a map she was using in social studies. Thus, the student got supportive instruction that she could apply directly in the classroom. I explained that *Nova* actually means "new" and *Scotia* referred to Scotland. When she identified the cluster of provinces, such as New Brunswick and Newfoundland, she was able to recall Nova Scotia as well, including the "scot" part of Nova Scotia. She was guided to see that many countries in Central America, such as Nicaragua and Guatemala, end with the letter *a*. This provided her with a memory strategy for spelling countries in this region. On a remedial level, we compared words similar in appearance like *Rico* and *Rica* (Puerto Rico and Costa Rica). I explained that the letter *i* can have the long *e* sound, particularly in names like *Rita*, *Rio*, and so forth.

HELPING JUGGLERS IN THE CLASSROOM

Some kids have a hard time shifting attention and/or trying to attend to several things simultaneously. That's where supportive note taking can help.

A class studied PowerPoint slides with views of a Holocaust museum, as well as views of Auschwitz and Mauthausen. Discussion, questioning, and exploration of the symbolic use of visual imagery took place simultaneously. My job was to take notes. The content was emotionally charged and important on many levels. The students needed to look closely, compare, talk, listen, recall, and reflect. That's a lot to juggle if you add paper and pencil. By taking notes, I removed one item from the mix.

Some people are masterful at juggling several tasks and shifting attention. They're often identified as skillful multitaskers. The ability to manage several modalities (visual, auditory, motor) simultaneously is often referred to as integration.

SUMMARY

A learning specialist serves in a variety of capacities to ensure proper service delivery to students with documented needs. Rarely involved in the formal aspects of diagnosis, a learning specialist focuses on support. This may involve direct service, such as teaching a student how to expand writing using a specific strategy (see Chapter 6, "Writing and Pancakes").

In addition, the learning specialist facilitates accommodations such as reading or scribing for students. Quite often, a learning specialist supervises a group of students who require extended time on tests.

Beyond direct service and accommodations, a learning support program can provide such commodities as recorded books, AlphaSmarts or laptop computers, Penned Notes (see Chapter 5) for note takers, and duplicate texts or supplies for students with documented organizational difficulties (see Chapter 7). Also, the program may provide resources for professional development, including a small library of books and/or DVDs.

One of the most valuable functions provided by a program of support is consultation. Sharing knowledge about special needs, creating an atmosphere of acceptance, and supporting faculty all contribute to a climate of acceptance. In such an atmosphere, students are more likely to feel comfortable about their differences. Eventually, they may be ready to advocate for themselves. In some educational settings, students without documentation may come to a study hall asking for help on a specific task. Within a climate of acceptance, teachers are more likely to request information and support. They may ask for an AlphaSmart or a stack of Penned

Notes to keep in their classroom. Finally, given a climate of trust and acceptance, parents are more likely to bring concerns and questions to school. They may inquire about support groups (see Resources at the end of this book), tutors, psychologists who conduct evaluations, counselors, or speech and language specialists.

5 Accommodations
Adjustments That Work

Accommodations require an evaluation. Students are not offered accommodations unless there is documentation of need in the form of a written report that summarizes the results of an evaluation. Many parents and some students are eager to have certain accommodations, such as extended time on the SAT or ACT. The intention of providing a student with an accommodation, however, is to level the playing field. The proper and appropriate use of accommodations never gives an advantage but rather keeps a student from being penalized due to a proven disability. For example, if a student is known to process information slowly, it is appropriate to offer him extended time so that he will not be penalized for difficulties with processing speed.

Accommodations place a lot of responsibility on the student. For example, it is not uncommon for a student with attentional difficulties to receive the accommodation of extended time on tests—that is, the student will have additional supervised time to complete tests. For students with ADHD, remaining seated longer than other students can be very challenging; however, many students persevere to finish the test.

In many public school systems, when test results confirm a student's need, there is an extensive menu of accommodations. The key to helping the student manage the disability is the consistent and positive provision of accommodations. Some students will be comfortable advocating for themselves; however, many do not achieve this level of acceptance until the college years. Therefore, it will be necessary for the parents and/or learning specialist to make sure that teachers understand the reasons for the accommodations and that they implement them accordingly.

Naturally, findings in the evaluation are of little value unless there is good follow-through with support and accommodations. It is wise to set up a conference between the parents and teachers a week prior to the beginning of a trimester/semester to clarify necessary accommodations. If the student is in ninth grade or higher, it can be valuable to have her attend this conference. In addition, it can be worthwhile having the examiner who did the testing attend the conference, particularly in cases where the school seems unfamiliar with implementing accommodations. The student, teacher, and parents need to be on the same page in terms of expectations about service delivery.

THE WHY OF ACCOMMODATIONS

A student is entitled to accommodations as specified in a Student Learning Plan or IEP because doing so is mandated by law. The Americans with Disabilities Act states that if the following conditions are met, accommodations must be made:

1. The student's needs are well documented (evaluation 3 years old or fewer), with accommodations/supports specifically stated in the report.

2. The accommodations are "reasonable."

3. The accommodations do not alter programs fundamental to the school (i.e., the accommodations are mission oriented).

4. The accommodations do not place an undue burden on the school (e.g., financial, personnel).

ART MUSEUMS

Art museums offer guided audio tours. I'm so grateful they do. If I hadn't been provided the background and a helpful audio tour, Picasso's *Guernica* would have just seemed like an unattractive canvas to me. I needed someone to point out the issues I was missing. I needed someone to spell it out for me. The truth: I needed to be "spoon-fed." Then, I had an understanding and appreciation.

Most students will understand and appreciate literature if teachers provide them with background information. Understanding aspects of the author's life and purpose in writing, key vocabulary terms, and specific literary devices will enhance students' comprehension of literature. Teachers need to guide students, and certain students will need much guidance. Teachers should be ready to "spoon-feed" students who are concrete thinkers or who struggle to read.

HOW LONG TO ACCOMMODATE?

How long should a student be provided accommodations?

Won't he or she outgrow the disability?

Isn't the support just a crutch?

These are some of the questions that come up fairly routinely once a student is identified as having special needs. In my experience, a student may learn compensatory strategies over time and cope better than before he or she was diagnosed. As material becomes more difficult and the pace and competitive nature of educational programs accelerate, however, compensation is usually not enough. In addition, unless a student is diagnosed with a chronic disability (e.g., hearing loss), he or she is required to have the evaluation updated every 3 years to determine if the accommodations and supports continue to be justified. Legally, if a student has documentation of need (a solid evaluation with recommendations supported by findings), demonstrates this need in an academic setting ("functional limitation"), and uses the accommodations/supports to his or her benefit within that setting, one cannot withdraw accommodations or supports. If the student, teachers, and parents agree to "test the waters" without supports and accommodations, I would suggest recording this agreement in writing, such as via a parent contract. If the student no longer needs the supports and/or accommodations, the functional limitation would not be relevant. The risk is that the student's ability to access accommodations could be questioned in the long run, and it is always possible that under stress, a student might need to reactivate these supports.

As far as the "crutch" question goes, it's like asking, "Will my eyesight improve if I take off my glasses?" As in any situation, a student might abuse the system. He or she (or his or her parents) could be intent on obtaining every accommodation as frequently as possible. I don't think this is common. Most students would rather function without the support than with it.

The fact that virtually all colleges, universities, and graduate programs offer many accommodations for students with disabilities supports the position that learning disabilities continue to present significant obstacles to many students in educational settings well beyond high school.

NO FEAR SHAKESPEARE

Many students can read literature. They may even enjoy it. Yet, they may not be able to understand abstract symbolic meaning. They are concrete thinkers. Shakespearean drama, *Beowulf*, and the like will probably be beyond their grasp without a guide. These students need a teacher- or commercially prepared guide, such as SparkNotes or No Fear Shakespeare. If there is a pervasive, pronounced verbal learning disability, these students may stumble through complex material and get little beyond frustration and bewilderment. One alternative is to give them a guide that may help them see what they otherwise would have missed. Mind you, I believe it would be against any reasonable system of ethics to have students with learning disabilities read the prepared notes in lieu of the original. A student with a learning disability would have to read more, not less. I know this is controversial. Still, I hope all readers will try to imagine the dilemma of a student with a pronounced reading disability.

If your choices are

1. read the original and gain little from it, or

2. read the original, gain little from it, and then read the prepared notes and gain a lot more,

wouldn't you pick Number 2?

BUSINESS CLASS FOR ALL

Copying is an assumed skill. It's part of a vast fund of knowledge that teachers quite naturally take for granted.

For example, many students do not copy accurately due to difficulties with pace, attention, visual-motor integration, visual perception, and so forth. As a result, spacing becomes an important feature on worksheets and tests. On a test, teachers don't expect to be evaluating how accurately a student copies. They are looking for the student's mastery of concepts and skills.

If a student is to write an answer on a prepared sheet, to plan the space needed, consider the student with the largest handwriting as opposed to the "average" size handwriting. This consideration is especially important for math computation. Students working a math problem in a cramped space are at a disadvantage, but so are students who must copy a problem onto another sheet of paper. Be sure to provide enough space.

MANAGING DYSGRAPHIA

Several approaches are very effective in limiting the impact of dysgraphia on a student's written performance. In addition, they are easy to implement in most educational settings. Technology has opened a lot of doors for students with writing difficulties. Recommended interventions often include the following:

- Using the word processor
- Using an AlphaSmart or laptop for taking notes in class
- Getting an extra set of notes from a buddy (see "Penned Notes" on p. 43)
- Having extra time on tests that involve a significant writing component
- Using shortcuts, such as standard abbreviations
- Using strikethroughs instead of erasures

The following accommodations are a bit more complicated and costly to implement but also valuable:

- Using voice-activated software (e.g., Dragon NaturallySpeaking)
- Arranging for a scribe to record work or answers

A BIG DIFFERENCE

A student in 11th grade had an evaluation done. Among other things, the findings showed that he had significant difficulties with pace. Therefore, it was recommended that he be given additional time to complete quizzes, tests, exams, and standardized tests, such as the SAT and ACT. The recommendation was made for "untimed" testing. This terminology is a bit misleading. At present, "untimed" time actually means double time, and "extended" time actually means time and a half.

How much of a difference could this accommodation make? In his case, it made a tremendous difference. The examiner administered several subtests with and without time constraints. The difference in many key subject areas was an astonishing eight grade levels. Later, the student took the SAT with extended time, and his scores increased by 150 points.

PROVIDE VERSUS OFFER

Regarding accommodation on tests, there's a difference between providing the accommodation and offering the accommodation. For students who are new to the system, new to the school, or just young, the difference can be significant.

Offer might look/sound like this:

A teacher speaks privately to a student: "Remember, you can have additional time on this test if you want."

Provide might look/sound like this:

A teacher speaks privately to a student: "You can have extended time on tests. I've made arrangements with the learning specialist to have you take the test in her room."
     or
"I want you to take the time you need to do well, so I've made arrangements for you to take this test in a quiet room with . . ."

- When extended time is offered, the student makes the choice.
- When extended time is provided, the student has little choice.

In early adolescence, when the need to fit in is strong, students may hurry just to complete the test like everybody else. If students choose not to use extended time, they can't know if the accommodation will make a difference.

If they rarely use extended time, this decision will hinder development of acceptance and perhaps the ability to advocate for their own learning needs. In the long run, a student who rarely uses extended time may find himself ineligible for accommodations on standardized tests. On the Independent School Entrance Examination (ISEE), SAT, and ACT, "nonstandard" administration takes place in a separate location from "standard" administration. Schools and students have to be very intentional about filling out paperwork and providing the accommodation.

USE IT OR LOSE IT!

The procedures and policies that determine a student's eligibility for accommodations on standardized tests (e.g., SAT, ACT) have tightened up over the years. Students need a recent evaluation documenting needs; however, if the student has been successful in her current educational setting without using testing accommodations on a regular basis (especially over the 6 months prior to a high-stakes test), she will probably not be found eligible for accommodations. This looks like a "use it or lose it" situation. A student who comes to grips with her differences, accepts them, and advocates for herself will have the edge here. Congratulations to those students who have the courage and persistence to get what they need and deserve.

TABLE OR BOOTH?

At a restaurant, the waiter offers a choice of a table or a booth. Which is preferred? My guess is the booth. A booth helps screen out extraneous stimuli (auditory and visual) and enables the diner to remain focused. A booth is also more private and comforting. For students who struggle with attentional difficulties and/or anxiety, a boothlike environment works best. That is why some students take tests in the learning specialist's office. It is generally more private and quiet. Certain students may even qualify for a private room for standardized testing.

HEAR THIS!

Listening to words makes them come alive. Some students experience reading as simply driving their eyes across the page. When they reach the bottom of a page, they have no idea what they read. For certain students, voices and print are much more effective than print alone. The solution is books on tape.

This support can help students with

- Reading fluency problems,
- Significant decoding issues,
- Long commutes to school and spending a lot of time in the car,
- Busy schedules with multiple responsibilities
- Limited receptive vocabulary, and
- Attentional difficulties.

Teachers can order tapes or CDs for key literary pieces. These can be reused year after year. Perhaps some fluent student readers with dramatic talent and clear diction would be willing to record a chapter or two in a book. It could be a great experience for the reader, and it would be a great gift to others. Some students may qualify for RFB&D (whose Web site is noted at the end of this book).

PENNED NOTES

Penned Notes are carbonless copy sets. Two sheets of paper, each a different color, are attached at the top by a gentle adhesive. During note taking, someone takes notes and then separates the two sheets when the note taking is complete. The system works best when a pen is used—hence, the name. The note taker (scribe) can keep the top sheet for herself and give the bottom sheet to another student or the teacher. Some teachers keep a complete set of Penned Notes in their room for students who

- Are absent,
- Misplace notes,
- Have documented difficulties with handwriting, and/or
- Have documented difficulties with attention.

Some teachers scan Penned Notes and then post them using such software as Blackboard so the whole class can access them.

The copy sets can be ordered through rapid printing services. Don't ask for Penned Notes—that's just a name I coined for easy reference. Ask for copy sets. Design them any way that works for students. I designed them with a wide margin, wide lines, and headings (Date, Subject, Student, Page) and three-hole-punched them for binders.

Sometimes, I take Penned Notes to a meeting if I know a colleague is unable to attend.

LIST OF COMMON ACCOMMODATIONS

As technology advances, the list of assistive tools will lengthen. In the meantime, this list encompasses some of the most commonly implemented accommodations.

Classroom Setting

Reserve seat in a place where the student is near the board and the teacher.

Place student away from distractions that are notable inside and outside the classroom.

Instruction

Allow student to hear printed material using a reader or recording or by accessing a print-to-speech program.

Enlarge print (especially primary source material).

For spoken presentations, record lesson and supply student with the tape.

Read printed directions aloud to student.

Student Response

Allow written responses to be produced using a word processor or AlphaSmart.

Arrange to have the student dictate to a scribe.

Give student access to a speech-to-print program and a computer outfitted accordingly.

Photocopy answer sheet so student can record directly on the photocopied answer sheet, instead of having to record on a different sheet.

Permit student to dictate answers into a recorder (Dictaphone or other).

Authorize verbal as opposed to written responses.

Arrange for another student to take notes (Penned Notes).

Test Format

Limit the number of items on a page, leaving plenty of space between questions (especially calculations).

Use one side of page only.

Enlarge print.

Test Setting (Timing and Place)

Provide up to 100% extra time for test completion.

Allow student to take test in a different environment with fewer distractions.

Permit student to use noise-canceling headphones.

Schedule testing with breaks, in multiple sessions, or on several different days.

Other

Give student frequent breaks.

SUMMARY

Learning about accommodations inevitably involves understanding why the accommodations are appropriate and reasonable. Very rarely will students be given accommodations without documentation. Occasionally, in private schools, students may be given accommodations to observe the student's response. In this sense, the accommodation is being used in a diagnostic-prescriptive manner. For example, if extended time improves a student's performance greatly, it may be wise to pursue an evaluation.

Different institutions scrutinize the rationale for accommodations more closely than others. Notably, it is crucial to remain current about documentation that meets criteria established by the board of the SAT. This information can be accessed online; however, anyone interested in applying for nonstandardized administration of the SAT must plan far in advance of the deadline. A year or so should be allowed in case an appeal is needed. As indicated in this chapter, accommodations on the SAT may improve a student's score considerably.

Writing difficulties can be quite easily accommodated given advancements in technology; however, the student's keyboarding skills should be strong to yield maximum benefits from laptops and AlphaSmarts. Speech-to-print software is also available for those with strong reading, verbal fluency, and dictation skills. To use such programs to their best advantage, the student will need to spend considerable time training the computer to recognize his voice. For example, Dragon NaturallySpeaking Preferred can help a high school student complete a written assignment very quickly. Copy sets, such as those described under "Penned Notes" above, can provide clear note-taking support for a student with writing difficulties. Many colleges provide notes online for all students in class.

Reading difficulties are a challenge to manage at upper levels due to the volume of reading assignments. Recorded books are available, and some students may qualify for materials through RFB&D. Listening takes a good deal longer than silent reading, so time management will be important if the student relies on recordings. Beyond mitigating a reading disability, there are benefits to recorded material. Listening to a book on tape improves comprehension, appreciation, and even memory for material.

Technology has developed the ability to use print-to-speech programs, such as the Kurzweil and Wynn 3. These devices are costly and limited in number, even at the university level. Students using these instruments and programs will need excellent time management, as books will need to be scanned prior to using the technology and listening to the book.

The program for students with learning disabilities will play an active role in facilitating accommodations. In higher education, student acceptance will be crucial to success since the student must be willing to visit and work with specialists in a department, such as Disability Support Services.

6 Strategies

Practical Tips to Help Students

I n the sequence of helping a struggling student, at this point, information about the student's needs is available and understood. Classroom teachers have been consulted and are aware and sensitive to the issues. Accommodations are in place. Now, one of the key questions arises: What specifically can be used to address student needs in the classroom, as well as in small-group or individual lessons? This section—about the approaches, tips, and practical ways to improve students' learning, memory, response, and overall functioning—might well be considered the meat and potatoes of this book.

The strategies have been broken down into skill categories. Students with different disabilities can exhibit similar skill deficits; therefore, strategies within skill sections are applicable to students who may have different diagnoses. For example, students may have difficulty sustaining attention because they have anxiety or ADHD. Still, the approaches noted under the skill section for "attention" will be applicable for students with either deficit.

Some of the approaches ask teachers to adjust their style of teaching a bit. For example, a dramatic approach that involves exaggeration may make the strongest impression. Other times, a more soothing, quiet manner may be most appropriate for the task. It will be up to individual teachers to know the task, understand their students' needs, and certainly develop a comfort zone for various approaches.

I suggest you record any strategies that you have seen or heard from colleagues or at conferences. Remaining open to change and trying new techniques can be the greatest gifts from teachers to students.

STRATEGIES THAT ADDRESS DIFFICULTIES WITH *ATTENTION*

Hear Yourself Think

The phrase "I can't hear myself think" describes a frustrating situation. Being in this state is uncomfortable, as if the stimuli on both sides of a person's head have merged and are too much to handle simultaneously.

Sometimes, the distractions are external, such as a passing lawn mower or laughter outside the room; sometimes, the distracters are internal, including preoccupations like "What if I get sick again?" "I hope my dog is OK today," and "Will I get invited to the party?"

First, I try to turn up the volume on the thinking part. I encourage students to think out loud. The auditory feedback helps enormously with planning, pace, sequencing, sustained attention, and need for clarification. For example, it helps greatly when a student can talk through the steps of long division, such as "First, I divide. Four goes into 27 six times, so that's 24. Now, I subtract. Twenty-seven minus 24 is 3. Now, I compare 3 to the divisor, and it's lower than 4—good. Next, I bring down the 2. That makes 32. Now, I divide again. Four goes into 32 eight times. Now, I subtract— bingo! I got 0, so that's an even quotient of 68." Naturally, this type of vocalization calls for a private setting. I encourage students to whisper, and eventually, the whisper can fade into a subvocalization.

If the volume on the thinking part can't be turned up, try turning down the volume on the other stimuli. White noise, earplugs, noise-canceling headphones, or music can help. Curiously, closing one's eyes can help too, even though this limits visual stimuli only. Deep breathing and visualization techniques may help with internal preoccupation that is creating anxiety.

Sound of Silence

I was working with a group of students who were quite chatty. Instead of asking them to stop talking, I asked them to start listening. I instructed them to see how many distinct environmental sounds they could identify. The class was silent. They identified the following:

- Lockers closing
- Fans blowing
- Papers shuffling
- Overhead lights buzzing
- Wind rustling leaves outside

- Eraser squeaking on whiteboard
- Caps coming off markers
- Teachers speaking in adjacent classroom

This task provides a nice break in teaching and helps prime students' listening skills for the major task at hand. It also requires silence without specifically demanding it.

Emergency Treatment for Chatty Classes

This strategy may be controversial, but it works well for me when I am teaching a class, and the students tell me they like it.

1. I ask students to tell me what time the class period ends (even though I already know the answer).

2. I record this time on the board so all can see.

3. I explain that I understand they want to talk with each other; however, teaching comes first. I say that class will end 4 minutes early to give students time to talk.

4. I change the time on the board to reflect 4 minutes for talking

5. I further explain that since there is now a designated time for talking, I will not permit any talking whatsoever while I am teaching. Questions and relevant comments require raised hands. The consequence of any talking will be an adjustment in the time class ends.

6. If there is any talking, I immediately (and without comment) go to the board, erase the projected time for end of class, and add 1 minute (class is longer). This usually happens once and rarely twice.

7. If I perceive that all students are giving me rapt attention, I may go to the board, erase the projected time for end of class, and subtract a minute.

Outcome

Students immediately get the relationship between talking and loss of "free time." I get to teach uninterrupted, and students get to learn without interruption. The "customary and usual" 4 minutes spent quieting/correcting kids in class are unnecessary. The stress level is remarkably low.

Recording Blanks

When students are taking notes, sometimes they may get distracted, tired, a fierce itch, a loose contact lens, or whatever. I suggest the following to manage this:

- Skip several lines to provide space for fill-in later.
- Mark CBL (for come back later).
- Quickly glance around to see who did *not* miss this information and jot their initials in the space.

Resulting notes might look like this:

- Armies in the Civil War . . .
- CBL see J. F. for notes
- Battles in the Civil War . . .

Mostly Listening With a Chance of Discussion

Climates in classrooms are almost as changeable as those in the outdoors. One day brings a torrent of discussion in which students are expected to participate. The next day brings a drought where even a spark of conversation seems like a deluge.

Many children are not able to accurately predict the classroom climate. Teachers can help by providing a forecast. It might be helpful to gauge expected participation as indicated on the scale from 1 to 10.

At the beginning of class, state clear expectations for student participation. For example, "Today will be a 3. Yesterday was an 8, so be prepared for this change in the classroom climate and my expectation." Discuss the different levels of listening and speaking. Consider how responses might differ between

- A class that offers a review for a test and
- A class that introduces new information.

Student response involves a range of any of the following:

- Sustained listening
- Quickly alternating listening and contributing
- Sustained listening and note taking (80/20)
- Listening in chunks and responding in chunks
- Questions only (hand raised)

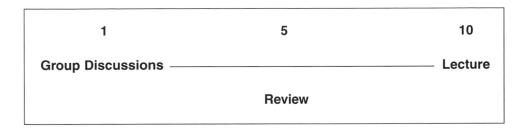

1	5	10
Group Discussions ——————————————— Lecture		
	Review	

Lights Out!

When writing at the computer, many students interrupt their own work to correct mechanical errors. This can be the effect of the high stimulus value of the monitor or the child's inability to inhibit or delay response to such stimuli. Often, students are preoccupied with the green lines that pop up and jump to correct each mistake as it appears. This is a very inefficient way of writing and does not allow the students' thoughts to flow. A simple solution to this frequent shifting of gears between writing and editing is to turn off the monitor. This change takes a bit of adjustment for some students, but it's certainly worth a try—or five tries. Encourage writing in layers. Type, type, type, and then edit, edit, edit.

STRATEGIES THAT ADDRESS DIFFICULTIES WITH *MEMORY*

Fading

Fading is a study technique that can support memorization. The catch is that the models need to be written by someone other than the student. The example below involves learning to spell *Baghdad*.

- The model (completed by someone other than the student) is written clearly in fairly large letters (Number 1).
- The student takes an index card in hand, looks carefully at the model, and says the letters out loud, which is important throughout this technique.
- Next, the student slides his index card down to cover Step 1 and goes on to Step 2, saying and writing the missing letter.
- This is repeated for the remaining numbers.

- By Step 8, the complete spelling of *Baghdad* is required.
  1. Baghdad
  2. Baghda_
  3. Baghd_ _
  4. Bagh_ _ _
  5. Bag_ _ _ _
  6. Ba_ _ _ _ _
  7. B_ _ _ _ _ _
  8. _ _ _ _ _ _ _

Mnemonics are a form of fading. So is alternating recitation, which can work well for memorizing pieces to be recited. I start reciting the piece and stop at a certain point, which can be random. The student continues to recite the piece until I interrupt him, and the process cycles through. This can help students who, when derailed, have to start all over from the beginning. Technically, I'm calling on students to use context and closure.

Adding Sensory Feedback to Flashcards

When struggling to recall information from a text, students often remark, "I remember this was at the top of the left page." For some learners, it's easy to recall position in space. This link often leads to full memory of the item. Kinesthetic and auditory cues can help with memory. When looking for my misplaced keys, I will often coach myself to think, "Where do I remember holding my keys?" I'm trying to tap into my kinesthetic recall. "Do I recall a sound that they made when landing on a surface?" With this question, I am exploring auditory memory.

Where do you keep your keys? Do you remember the feeling of placing them in that spot? Do you remember how they sound when they land in that spot?

Adding sensory impact to flashcards can facilitate memorization. Try the following:

1. Have the student fold flashcards in the middle of the longest side. I call this a "tent" fold.

2. Stand flashcards in a line along the edge of a table. Coach the student to recite the information out loud and fold the flashcard inside out after the recitation is complete.

3. Have him or her move systematically along the line of flashcards from left to right.

After several repetitions, the student will probably be able to tell you which facts/vocabulary terms are located on the ends (left or right), which are in the middle, etc.

This same principle can be done by taping flashcards on cabinet doors (inside or out). This will give the student a chance to step along the sequence and perhaps open and close doors. This would work well for students who need movement.

Envelope Sort

This is a memorization technique that works well for students who have good spatial awareness and those who like to move around the room. It works best for discrete units of information associated with several characteristics, such as categorization tasks. Here is an example from science:

Kingdom Plantae	*Kingdom Fungi*	*Kingdom Eubacterial*
multicellular	multicellular	unicellular
eukaryotes	eukaryotes	prokaryotes
producers	decomposers	producers and consumers (including decomposers)

Materials Needed

- Index cards
- Envelopes
- Tape
- Pen and pencil
- Scissors
- A surface/wall where it's OK to tape things

Method

1. Get or make three envelopes for the three categories.

2. Write the name of each category (kingdom) under the opening/flap of each envelope.

3. Tape three envelopes on the wall (close together for older kids, farther apart for younger kids or those who need more movement).

4. Write each characteristic (e.g., multicellular) on one line of an index card, and skip two lines between each characteristic.

5. Cut characteristics apart into strips. Several strips will name the same characteristic (e.g., producers, multicellular, and eukaryotes), so expect some duplicate strips.

6. Sort characteristics by placing them into envelopes.

7. When all the strips have been placed inside envelopes, see if students can tell you what's inside each envelope.

8. Check by taking strips out of envelopes.

9. Shuffle the strips and sort them again.

Mistakes That Help

Tease out meaning from letters, words, and symbols by using concocted names and/or spellings, for example:

"adverbly" for *adverb*

"wubble you" for the letter name of *W*

"yi" for the letter name of *Y*

"upostrophe" for *apostrophe*

"verbicate" for *predicate*

Brain research shows that connecting positive emotions to learning can make learning stick. According to Priscilla Vail (2007), a prominent national educator, an esteemed author, and an expert in learning disabilities, dyslexia, and giftedness, "The emotional brain, the limbic system, has the power to open or close access to learning, memory, and the ability to make novel connections." I hope that silliness and humor will work with the concocted terms above.

Flying Apostrophe

Symbols are often squiggles identical in every way except position in space. Many children can't remember the names of these squiggles, so I suggest a brief cartooning lesson. Once, a very logical student asked about the placement of curls: "Why isn't a comma called a 'downostrophe' since the apostrophe is positioned up?" What a great question!

Teachers should feel free to ham it up to help with name recall, as well as position in space, for these bizarre squiggles of punctuation. I've chosen to have the comma offer a courteous curtsy so he or she remains grounded (starts on the line), but the action of curtsying requires him or her to "dip" below the line. The flying apostrophe has an adventurous and risk-taking side to him or her—a bit like an acrobat. Put a cape on the apostrophe, and he or she swings in thin air.

Environmental Cues

For a class involving map study skills, teacher-developed materials may be placed in folders in the classroom. The materials will be readily available, and the folders will provide a concrete visual reminder of the lesson.

For a class involving test preparation, a basket with test-preparation accoutrements, such as index cards and a mini list of strategies, could be kept out in the classroom.

Auditory stimuli vanish and are highly dependent on attention.

Environmental cues can refresh memory, as well as help students develop a more intentional approach to their work habits.

Preparing for a test? Go to the basket.

Studying a map? Go to the folders at the front of the room.

Establishing environmental cues in the classroom is common in lower school but less so in higher grades. Put surprises in cue containers at random times to encourage repeat visitors. How about miniature Tootsie Rolls in test-preparation baskets?

Out of sight, out of mind?

Cutting for Comprehension

Memorizing vocabulary is a common task for students. The definition often includes details that can detract from key elements that give meaning to the word. Guide students to delete unnecessary words, especially articles (e.g., *the, a, an*). Students can always add these words back in if needed. Have students use abbreviations (e.g., "nat'l" for *national*), numerals (e.g., 2 instead of *two*), and symbols, such as the ampersand (i.e., & for *and*). Where possible, students may also substitute simpler words for those in the definition. The final result of these adjustments will make the task of memorization simpler, and students will be able to focus on the most meaningful parts of the definition. This is essentially the beginning of note-taking skill development.

Consider the following for the vocabulary item "loose construction":

Original definition: An interpretation of the Constitution that argues that the government can do anything the Constitution does not plainly forbid it to do

After cutting for comprehension: Interpret. of Constit. says gov't can do anything Constit. doesn't forbid

Another example uses the definition for the vocabulary item "opposites" (math):

Original definition: Two numbers that are the same distance from zero on the number line but in opposite directions

After cutting for comprehension: 2 nos. = same distance from 0 on NL but in opposite directions

What's in a Name?

I designate techniques using specific names. Some of these names are well recognized (e.g., chunking), and others are invented (e.g., fading). In general, it seems that students are more likely to recall and use something defined by a name. The names I use include fading, chunking, and 1–2–3. Providing names can also save teaching time. For example, a teacher might say,

- "I suggest chunking this material for memorization."
- "Use fading if the spelling is difficult for you."
- "Since you've got quite a bit for homework, be sure to use 1–2–3 prioritization for the vocabulary test."

Minimal Pairs

This term refers to two units of information that have very similar structures. One or two key features distinguish the items. Comparing and contrasting minimal pairs can improve attention to visual detail. Some examples of minimal pairs include:

- Text; test
- Proposition; preposition
- Checks on the president by Congress; checks by the president on Congress
- 4 times the sum of a number and 15 is equal to 80; 4 times a number and 15 is equal to 80
- 80.4; 8.40

The most challenging minimal pairs have differences in the middle of the expression. Attending to interior visual detail does not come easily to most of us. Examining and discussing the differences can be enlightening.

Talking to Yourself Is a Good Thing!

I've heard it said that people who talk to themselves are "crazy." I don't agree. Thinking out loud (vocalization) or "inside your head" (subvocalization) is an effective coping strategy for people with short-term memory difficulties and/or attentional problems. This technique is sometimes referred to as self-talk. The addition of an auditory component to an otherwise purely mental task adds a sense of intention, as well as the auditory modality. Some people use self-talk automatically:

> "Let's see, today is Day 4, it's fifth period, and that means I have . . . aha, science."

Students with organizational difficulties can benefit from specific scripts, such as,

> "My next class is_____, so I'll need to take my _____."

> "Before I leave the room, let me check around my desk for my materials."

Students with mild performance anxiety may be able to keep their worries in check with affirming self-talk, such as,

> "I can handle this."

Multistep math problems lend themselves to subvocalization. For example, managing regrouping for addition is a snap with scripts like

> "Put down the _____ and carry the ____."

Working Memory

Working memory is a very practical aspect of memory. Many students who struggle with sustained attention also have difficulties with working memory. Working memory is involved when a person is

- Holding a question in mind while formulating a response and listening to other student responses. Sometimes the student is called on, but by then, he has forgotten what he was going to say. This is mostly likely due to a problem with working memory.
- Holding in memory the various components of a task while completing that task. Consider the many steps in long division and proofreading.
- Flipping through the pages of a book, looking for the one page a teacher asked her to turn to.

What can be done to help a student with working memory issues?

- To gain time and help a student save face, practice role-playing and develop a response for moments when working memory issues occur. For example, "Can you come back to me? I need a minute to think."

Since working memory takes place in the mind, it's helpful to add visual and auditory cues. Try these strategies:

- Encourage self-talk. Hearing steps will guide the student through them.
- Encourage the student to jot abbreviations for steps (e.g., PEMDAS for the order of operations in math).
- Provide a checklist (e.g., for proofreading: capitals, punctuation, spelling, title, name, etc.).
- Suggest that a written piece be read aloud for proofreading.
- Tell the student to tick off steps on his fingers.

STRATEGIES THAT ADDRESS DIFFICULTIES WITH *NOTES*

Step Aside!

Delivering a lecture-style presentation, a teacher may require students to take notes using their choice of format. She may deliberately go off on tangents, and contribute bits and pieces of personal opinion and experiences to see if students can discern tangential from salient information.

If students have trouble discerning relevant information during lectures, a teacher could give a physical cue for tangents by moving to the side of the classroom. Stepping to the side can be a visual cue for any nonessential comments you wish to offer. It seems a bit like the difference between center stage and stage left or right.

Teachers often cue students with remarks like "I'm getting a bit off-track here." This is a valuable cue for verbal learners. It will help nonverbal learners if lecturers move from the center of the room to the side to signal nonessential information. Position in space can be a significant cue for visual and spatial learners.

Note Card No Man's Land

After many hours of research for a paper, a student is naturally delighted to have completed recording information on note cards. Next, it's time to sort them into categories to develop a sense of the subtopics. With cards in hand, the student sees the subtopics become clearer as the piles of related cards grow taller; however, the student often comes across a card that doesn't seem to fit in any of the existing piles. She has to decide on relevance and importance. Should she start a new pile? She reads the card silently at first and then out loud. Still, she wonders why this information is important. Why had she recorded it? Finally, she decides it is not worth including in the paper. She could discard it, but just for fun, she makes it the first card to be placed in a category called "Who Cares," or "Misfits." On lengthy assignments, there may be several cards in this pile.

Word Processing Index Cards

This technique may be useful for students with dysgraphia. Buy white cardstock, which is essentially thick paper. You'll want standard size, 8.5 by 11 inches. Set up your document on the word processor so the margins will approximate the size of the note card you want. Use "print preview" to check it. Feed paper in printer by hand since it's quite thick. After printing, cut, and you have word-processed index cards!

There are obvious advantages, such as neater cards, faster production of cards, and spell-checked cards. In addition, these note cards will be saved on the computer in case they tumble out of a binder or get lost at school.

Some new software seems to be emerging that tries to simplify note taking on index cards. Stay on the lookout for new and improved methods.

Laterality and Learning

To help students study for a Civil War test, I devised some charts that would consolidate information. Notes were systematically sorted into two categories and placed on distinct sides of the page with "NORTH" on the left and "SOUTH" on the right.

Some students can easily associate names and placement. Left-right recognition of and response to position in space is called laterality. Students may actually learn or recall facts based on their position in space. The thoughts running through the mind of a laterality learner might go something like this: "Oh, I remember this was on the left side, so it's a military strategy that was used by the North." Color could also provide another sensory cue here. Blue notes would be placed on the left and gray notes on the right.

Driving and Note Taking

The 80/20 principle refers to the listening/note-taking ratio. Students need to listen carefully while they judge when and what to record. It's a little like driving a stick shift in stop-and-go traffic. Drivers need to be able to idle in neutral and then quickly shift into gear and accelerate.

Beginning note takers need prompts, such as,

- "This part is important."
- "Take note of this please."

Establish a backup system for students with attentional problems or dysgraphia. Penned Notes would work well.

STRATEGIES THAT ADDRESS DIFFICULTIES WITH *READING*

Touch the Page

I've heard driving enthusiasts insist that it makes a huge difference to use a manual transmission so they can "connect" with the road in a special way. They claim they can feel it. I encourage students to touch the page. This practice

- Facilitates note taking, highlighting, and underlining.
- Simplifies visual tracking.
- Enhances comprehension.
- Improves accuracy when transferring information, such as copying equations or new terms.
- Increases sensory feedback, helping students stay focused.

Whether students touch the page with a pen, an eraser, the end of a pencil, an index card, their fingertips, or even a stick of gum, they are forced to connect with the material. This tactile connection builds memory for names or dates: "Oh, I remember King George. He was on the top of the right-hand page."

When I see a student sitting at a distance from the page with the book propped open in a hands-off fashion, I feel that she is missing something. She probably is. This is one of my all-time favorite strategies. Eventually, it can be used to develop skimming.

Reading Fluency

Be aware that it's difficult to develop fluency in students with reading difficulties. Many of these students learned to read by decoding the printed word sound by sound. Research supports this as one of the best methods of reading instruction for dyslexic students. Naturally, it's challenging to get a student to transition from perceiving a series of sounds and words to discerning words as a meaningful chunk of language. For this reason, many dyslexic students have a reader for major tests since fluency can affect comprehension. Try any or all of the following strategies, but be aware that it takes time to develop reading fluency.

- Approach this skill in a one-on-one lesson since the student will naturally feel quite self-conscious reading aloud in front of others.
- Practice reading poetry. The best type of poetry for this purpose has a strong rhyming pattern and/or strong rhythm.
- Practice reading dialogue. The reader can usually sense the conversational nature of the words, particularly if the book is contemporary.
- Review key concepts in grammar. Recognition of prepositional phrases and independent clauses can provide the key to reading meaningful chunks of language.
- Give permission to substitute an abbreviated nickname for a long name, for example, "Tut" for "Tutankhamen."
- Use professionally narrated books on tape. Hearing pauses and the use of expression can help model appropriate fluency.
- Model reading fluency by reading aloud to students on a regular basis. Students are never too old to appreciate and benefit from hearing proficient readers read aloud.

Friendly Font

The lowercase *a* in the Comic Sans font appears as it would in traditional manuscript handwriting.

This cannot be said of most fonts. There is clarity and simplicity to this font that makes it seem friendly. I recommend it to most students with learning difficulties. It would be valuable to use in developing a test to minimize anxiety as many students describe it as "friendly."

Vitamin P

Vitamin P is a powerful "antiplagerite": It requires paraphrasing. Paraphrasing involves both reading comprehension and expressive vocabulary. Having students paraphrase information from any subject is of value to their language development. This strategy is clearly applicable to any area of the curriculum at any grade level.

The How of How

Strategies are ways to learn. I think of them as the "how" of academics. Some strategies have fairly clear names. For example, "chunking" refers to the strategy of breaking a sizeable amount of information into smaller, more manageable units. Other strategies have names that are less obvious. The names for reading comprehension strategies are a bit nebulous. You can clarify the names by giving the student a script to memorize and subvocalize. English departments often offer clarification of strategies with scripts, such as those that follow:

Strategy	*Script*
Connect	"This character reminds me of . . ."
Visualize	"I can picture the setting . . ."
Question	"I wonder why . . ."
Predict	"In the next scene, I bet that . . ."

White in Black and Read

Many students tell me it's much easier to read from a computer monitor if the print is highlighted. When highlighted, letters and symbols are white against a black background. For students who have difficulty perceiving background from foreground, it's possible that print is clearer in the highlighted mode. This technique is worth trying, especially for students with visual perceptual difficulties or those who have spent significant time looking at the monitor.

Dates and Margins

In history, dates mentioned in the text are often placed on a timeline. I encourage students to do the same for assignment due dates. The left margin on paper makes a perfect spot for a vertical timeline. Many students do not see dates like February 1, 2005, when they are embedded in the text. Once the dates are set aside, however, they can be referenced more easily.

Compare the following two statements:

1. Representatives from seven states met on February 4, 1861, in Montgomery, Alabama, and drew up a constitution for a new nation called the Confederate States of America.

2. On February 4, 1861, representatives from seven states met in Montgomery, Alabama, and drew up a constitution for a new nation called the Confederate States of America.

Putting the date first helps this chronological feature stand out.

Active Voice

It's extremely helpful for students to hear what is on a page. The material needs to be read aloud. When I'm working with dyslexic students, I want to emphasize their active involvement with printed material. I word my questions to empower them in terms of choices related to the printed word. Instead of presenting the choice as "Do you want to read, or do you want me to read?" I'll offer, "Do you want to read or listen?" Small change, big difference.

Readability: Little Things Mean a Lot

There are a number of ways to measure the reading expectancy level for books and other printed matter. The key factors used to determine readability are

- Legibility of print, including the type. Fluent readers rely on the upper coastline of print and the right-hand side of letters.
- Layout, including size of type, length of line, and spacing between the lines. Very long or short lines lead to inefficient eye movements.

A simple suggestion: Enlarge the size of the font and increase the space between lines; reading accuracy, fluency, and comprehension are all likely to improve. This topic is addressed more in the chapter on test format (Chapter 8).

Layout and Memory

A student was trying to memorize a piece to be recited before an audience. He has a strong memory for the "big picture." His gestalt kind of mind helps him a lot, but he can get lost in the details.

I decided to alter the layout of the original piece he was committing to memory so each thought was on one line. This way, the visual details of specific words were evident, and the entire thought was clear to him. This technique supports comprehension, as well as memory.

It's gen-

erally a lot har-

der to

figure things

out when

they are all

chopped up.

Newspapers are very challenging for students as illustrated by the phrase above. The column layout is a problem. For current events and editorials, I steer students toward *Time* or *Newsweek*.

Can They Read the Text?

Standardized testing can offer information about silent reading skills. Another practical assessment is oral reading in class. This can be tricky since students with fluency issues are naturally self-conscious about reading in front of their peers. Obviously, oral reading is not the same as silent reading. Try the following to see how well students actually decode the material assigned.

1. Reassure students that this activity will not be graded and is confidential.

2. Select a page from one of the current texts.

3. Tell the students to put their initials at the top of a sheet of lined paper.

4. Instruct them to make three columns on the paper. Have them label the left-hand column 1, the middle column 2, and the right-hand column 3.

5. Tell students that 1 refers to words that can be read with ease, 2 refers to words that took time to figure out, and 3 refers to words that could not be read.

6. Have students read a page or two silently. Require every student to put down at least 10 words. Some may have 10 words in column 1.

Column 3 will probably be longer for science and social studies readings where many of the words are actually new terms, often with a foreign base. Here is a sample from a social studies text.

1	2	3
nomad	petroleum	fjords
	nonrenewable	kimono
		drought
		geyser

I use this technique with older dyslexic students. I ask them to prepare a passage silently and jot words in columns. Then, I help them decode the 2s and 3s.

Music and Poetry

Key musical terms like *forte, pianissimo, andante,* and so forth give cues to the performer about interpretation and performance. I love the fact that a rest, or silence, is written for the instrumentalist or vocalist. The symbol for a rest is larger than a comma.

When reading poetry aloud, some students may benefit from the insertion of written cues. I suggest enlarging punctuation to make it stand out. Color-coding could be used to indicate style. Words intended to be given emphasis might be placed in bold or even capital letters. A simple drawing of an eye might indicate a good opportunity to establish eye contact with the audience.

Tachistoscope

Tachistoscope is a fancy name for an unlined index card/sheet of paper with a cutout in the shape of a small window. The size of the window can be customized or open-ended. When the window is placed over the problem/text being studied, this simple tool can help block out extraneous stimuli and increase attention to visual detail. A tachistoscope works well for students who

- Get anxious when they see lots of problems/questions on the page.
- Have trouble focusing on one item at a time.
- Experience visual perceptual problems and get confused with visually complex material.
- Have trouble copying/transferring material (nearpoint to nearpoint).
- Have trouble proofreading.

A student can create and personalize his or her own tachistoscope to make it more meaningful. Different sizes are needed for different-size fonts and symbols. On standardized tests, tachistoscopes can prevent students from skipping items and misaligning their answers.

People Are Round

Reading material that contains the names of foreign people and places can be confusing. I guide students to

- Circle the names of people, and
- Put a box around the names of places.

My corny rationale is that people are generally round and places are usually filled with box-shaped buildings.

This technique comes in handy for rapid location of names on an open-note test. It also makes reading more active and appeals to a nonverbal learner since specific shapes are involved.

Epic Management

A student was struggling to recall facts and understand a lengthy novel. She commented that she needed to reread the material frequently and was overwhelmed trying to keep up with other assignments. I suggested she try the following:

- Read the book out loud.
- Get a stack of sticky notes.
- Post a note on every third or fourth page of the reading.
- On each sticky note, jot notes about new developments in the plot, literary techniques, theme, and character development.

Initially, this technique will slow down reading since writing is added to the reading task; in the end, however, the strategy will eliminate the need to reread material. As the student develops familiarity with the characters and plot, she will be able to space out the use of sticky notes and quicken the pace. Adjust the number of pages between sticky notes according to the density of the material, as well as the student's abilities. If all the sticky notes are placed in order from first to last, the student will have her own "SparkNotes" for the book.

Jigsaw Puzzles and Research Projects

My friend is a jigsaw puzzle wizard. For her, looking at the picture on the front of the box is cheating. For me, this step is a necessity. I have to know what I'm trying to form to figure out where a piece might fit. If it's not a corner or a straight-edged piece. I have no clue what I'm looking at. Some diagnosticians will call this a part-whole issue.

I watch students researching. They locate information (the piece) but don't know its significance or place because they don't have knowledge of the whole. They may have to collect many pieces before they can perceive where and how each piece will fit.

Techniques to help researchers:

- Encourage them to read an encyclopedia entry first to get an overview of the topic.
- Coach them to jot subtopics or chapter headings in sequence as they occur in books on the topic.
- Give them a list of questions to help them target specific aspects of the topic. Usually, *who*, *what*, *where*, *when*, *why*, and *how* will be involved. Inevitably, teachers want to know the importance of a topic. Why does it matter? To whom does it matter?

Unstructured Texts

Unstructured texts have many fine qualities and often render material very readable. Such texts, however, may not provide certain aspects of structure that support comprehension, memory, and organization of material, including

- Chapter titles,
- Vocabulary items,
- Subheadings, and
- Charts and graphs.

In response to this need, I devised a table to help students jot key features from an unstructured text. It was specifically designed to facilitate note taking on a history text. In the table that follows, adjust the size of the boxes to allow for more or less student input.

CHAPTER TITLE **PAGES**
PEOPLE
PLACES
EVENTS
VOCABULARY
QUOTES
ILLUSTRATIONS, CHARTS, MAPS (that I found helpful)
SUMMARY
QUESTIONS I HAVE

STRATEGIES THAT ADDRESS DIFFICULTIES WITH *WRITING*

Pick It! Stick It!

Tense shift is one of the most common errors in writing. I have used "Pick It! Stick It!" to caution students at the start of a new written piece. They like the catchy phrase. I tell students to pick a tense and then stick with it throughout the piece. I have concrete thinkers or those with memory difficulties record the tense they picked in the top right-hand corner of the assignment. Writing down the tense makes the "picking" more intentional and provides an important visual reminder when the writing is done over several sittings. In cases where English is a second language, this strategy may have less effect in consistent application; however, at a minimum, it is likely to increase awareness.

Writing and Pancakes

Pour pancake batter on the griddle.
The bubbles appear, and then it's time to grab a spatula and flip it.
What happens next? The original small circle starts to expand.

I wanted a student to expand her written explanation of a situation. She came up with a few ideas but then drew a blank. I suggested she picture the "flip side" of the situation. She came up with more ideas and was able to apply them in reverse to her original explanation. For example:

How does the First Amendment affect the lives of American people?

Flip it: What kind of lives might Americans have without the First Amendment?

Write a Green Paragraph

Editing is often done in layers. The first round involves scanning for capitalization, the second round for spelling, and so forth.

For complex material, it may be best to read and write in layers. For example, consider reading and writing about several sociologists' commentaries on the social, political, and economic status of women in a certain culture at a certain time. This will be challenging. The text may not be structured to facilitate identification of the three concepts. Suggest to students that they read the material for one feature at a time. For example, on the first read, have students focus on economic status. Tell them to highlight key economic features in green. Then they can write a "green" paragraph. Next, have them read with an eye toward social issues and highlight them in orange. Then, they can write an "orange" paragraph. Finally, they can read through the material focusing on political views and highlighting them in blue. They can respond by writing a "blue" paragraph.

While reading in layers is time consuming, it actually facilitates comprehension, as well as clear writing. By the time students have read the material three times, they will have a clear understanding and be able to respond more completely.

Franklin Language Master

I have recommended this handheld electronic device for many students. I have one myself and like it.

What Is It?

A Franklin Language Master is a handheld, battery-operated electronic device with a miniature keyboard and small screen. Among other features, it can check spelling and has a dictionary and thesaurus. Some have a cartridge system to add features (e.g., foreign language). Some are voice synthesized. I think of it as a multifunction calculator for words.

Where Can You Get One?

Look for Franklin Language Masters at stores that carry portable electronic devices or school and office supplies.

How Much Does It Cost?

Franklin Language Masters cost about $20 to $130 depending on features.

What Kind of Students Benefit Most?

- Poor spellers who aren't using a word processor (Forget the dictionary.)
- Those with limited vocabulary
- Those who struggle to use a regular dictionary due to visual tracking problems
- Those with busy schedules or executive dysfunction who are often in a hurry

Prompts on the Computer

By the end of high school, the vast majority of students will have internalized the key elements of writing. Until that time, encourage students to put key elements in CAPITAL LETTERS in a Word document they could title "Writing template."

Students find it much simpler to respond to elements when they are visually represented. Once a student has written the element, he can delete the prompt in capitals. This system works almost like a template for an analytical essay. Students should check with their English teacher before and after developing a template, such as the following:

GRABBER

DETAILS

THESIS STATEMENT

TOPIC SENTENCE

TRANSITION

EXAMPLES

QUOTE FROM TEXT

CONCLUDING PARAGRAPH

Beat It!

Beat It! is a writing activity that involves competition. The goal is to improve the sentence by one or more elements (e.g., vocabulary or additional detail). Here is an example:

The first player writes:
    1. The dog ran.
The second player might "beat it" (Number 1) with:
    2. The dalmatian ran.
The first player might "beat it" with:
    3. The dalmatian puppy ran.
The second player might "beat it" with:
    4. The dalmatian puppy darted.

This can go on for quite a while. With the teacher's help, players should determine at which point the sentence has been adequately developed.

A teacher can also use "Beat It!" to convey to a student where her writing "fits" in the scheme of good writing. The teacher might say, "This looks like a Level 2 sentence. I'd like to have you bring it up to a Level 5. Consider your vocabulary, as well as additional details."

Boldly Stated

I encourage students to put their **thesis statements in bold**. This makes it easy for students to check if their writing supports their thesis. The bold comes off for the final copy.

Planned Ignoring of Written Mistakes

I acted as a scribe for a student who experienced significant difficulty getting ideas onto paper. I typed ideas as he articulated them. I noted that the student frequently used the pronouns *you* and *I* as he spoke. I was aware that this conversational style was not acceptable in his classroom. Yet, I allowed him to continue in this manner. I sensed that if I interrupted or corrected every *you* and *I*, the student's expressive fluency would have been reduced to a trickle. I simply ignored the mistakes for the time being. Once the thoughts were completed, I directed the student's attention to the use of *you* and *I* throughout the piece. We then worked to rephrase these sections.

Editing often occurs in layers. For students with significant difficulties, writing may need to be done in the same manner. As I continue to work with this student on writing, I hope he will automatically self-correct the pronoun usage. It will just take time.

Strikethrough

Deleting an error is easy on a word processor; however, if a student is working with a pencil, it's a multistep task. A task analysis reveals eight steps for an erasure:

1. Release thumb from pencil.

2. Invert pencil.

3. Establish new grip.

4. Hold paper firmly with nonwriting hand.

5. Rub eraser across error enough times to remove mark but not so many as to damage paper.

6. Flip pencil upright.

7. Rearrange grip.

8. Brush away eraser bits.

There's an easier way. Just use a strikethrough. A task analysis reveals two steps for a strikethrough:

1. Draw a line through the mistaken ~~item or items.~~

2. Write the correction next to it.

For students with fine motor issues who self-correct often, I strongly recommend strikethroughs as an alternative to erasing. The student won't lose time or momentum in his work. An additional benefit is that teachers will be able to see the number and type of self-corrections.

If a student struggles to finish assignments on time and uses many strikethroughs, it may be advisable to consider other options, such as using the word processor, arranging for a scribe, or reducing the length of assignments.

Puzzle Pieces

I was working with a student whose assignment was to write a response to a philosophical quote with two definite paragraphs:

- Paragraph 1: The meaning of the quote
- Paragraph 2: His interpretation of the quote

He had already jotted down some ideas before beginning to write. Some of his ideas did not seem to clearly belong to one or the other paragraph. He was stymied. I advised him to type undecided ideas between the paragraphs like this:

- Paragraph 1: Described meaning of quote blah blah blah blah
- Undecided ideas written here
- Paragraph 2: Interpretation of quote blah blah blah

Next, I suggested he compare the middle "undecided" paragraph with the other two paragraphs. Once all the ideas were recorded, it was easier for him to decide which paragraph was the better fit for the middle "undecided" portion. Then, he simply cut and pasted.

This technique is similar to pulling a single puzzle piece out of the box and comparing it with two puzzle sections that have already been started. Examine how the piece fits with existing sections. Which shape does it match most closely? Which color does it resemble? Now, put it together.

Struggling With Topic Sentence

Sometimes students can't generate a topic sentence. Part of this problem can be inertia. Part of it can be uncertainty and nerves. In these circumstances, I think it helps to put the topic sentence "on hold" and continue with the rest of the paragraph. Make the points first. Next, study the similarities between the points. Then, it is usually easier to form a topic sentence. Cap the points by emphasizing the common element.

Consider how a T is formed. First, the vertical line (symbolic for points) is usually formed. Next, the line is capped with a horizontal line (symbolic for topic sentence).

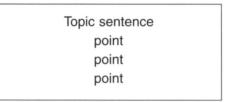

STRATEGIES THAT ADDRESS DIFFICULTIES WITH *MATH*

At First I Was Puzzled

When a student asked for clarification of a math question, I asked her to point to the confusing part of the question. She pointed to "a number m." Then, I realized that she (a slightly anxious and fairly concrete thinker) was probably wondering, "How can a number be a letter? How can you have a number m?" I substituted "a number called m" and made this change on the paper. She instantly understood. One word made the difference. Obviously, wording can significantly impact a student's interpretation of and response to a question. This topic is revisited in the chapter on test format.

Dramatizing Variables

I exaggerate when showing how to substitute for a variable. This is yet another instance when drama and emotion can make a process more memorable and enjoyable.

Example: Solve $2Y + 3$ when $Y = 7$.

Pretending to pinch the first Y and peel it off the page, I loudly proclaim, "I will pluck this Y off the page." I pretend to peel the Y off the text.

Then, I flick my wrist and toss the imaginary Y toward the wall as I declare with gusto, "I will fling the Y against the wall."

I pretend to follow the flying Y across the room and make a sound like "fump." There it is, gone from the equation. What can I put in its place to make this equation work? Ah, the 7!

Next, I pretend to pinch the 7 off the page and deposit it in its new home in the equation as I state, "Good thing we can use 7 as a substitute for Y."

The students take it from here with many amusing scenarios to demonstrate substitution.

Math and Margarine

Several years ago, there was an ad for a brand of margarine on television. The tub talked when the lid was lifted.

Scene—a kitchen
    Model holds a tub of margarine and asserts, "Margarine."
    She starts to pry the lid off the tub, and a voice from within the tub corrects her by saying, "Butter."
    Ah, the talking tub.

With fractions, I tell students that the line dividing the numerator from the denominator talks too. "Ah," the talking line exclaims, "divided by." I demonstrate with corny, high-pitched voices and really ham it up. Assuming students are reading fractions from top to bottom, when the talking line comes into play, 1 over 5 becomes 1 "divided by" 5, which can be calculated as 0.2.

There are many ways to change fractions to decimals. The talking line may help students remember one specific technique. It is especially appropriate for students who need a very concrete approach.

Which Way Does It Go?

Changing decimals to percents often confuses students. Here is a simple way to recall which direction to move the decimal point when changing decimals to percents and vice versa.

1. Write the alphabet.

2. Underline or circle the "d for decimal" and the "p for percent."

    a b c d̲ e f g h i j k l m n o p̲ q r s t u v w x y z

    This is the alphabet that will be used when figuring decimal point movement.

3. Now look at the first letters in the words *percent* and *decimal*: *p* and *d*.

4. To go from *decimal* to *percent*, move the point as if you were moving from *d* to *p* in the alphabet, which would be to the right.

5. To go from *percent* to *decimal*, move the point as if you were moving from *p* to *d* in the alphabet, which would be to the left.

Break an Arm

A student with a broken arm was sent by his teacher so I could scribe for a math test. He read every problem aloud and dictated every step of computation. This was not easy at first, but the step-by-step nature of vocalizing forced him to think out loud and slow down. His teacher later commented that on previous tests he had made careless errors. On this test, however, he earned an A. The mindset of having to be so intentional, deliberate, and stepwise worked to his benefit. Dictating forced the student to slow down and think out loud.

If "break a leg" ensures good luck for a performance, how about "break an arm" for a test?

Closer Look and Collaboration

An algebra teacher has a student with known learning disabilities that have been obvious in reading and writing; however, the problems have spilled over into math as well. When the teacher and I looked carefully at a sample problem, we saw the interference of visual perceptual difficulties.

Sample problem:

$3x + 9 = 12$

Since the symbol x is a rotated +, this could be confusing. It is likely to be more confusing because these symbols are next to each other in the equation. In addition, x can be a symbol of operation, so the student may not have perceived it as a variable.

Suggestions:

- Use a dot for multiplication. This is common practice.
- Substitute H (capital only). This letter cannot be reversed or inverted as x. Very rarely is the letter H rotated as an I, and then only in much younger children. The result is $3H + 9 = 12$.
- Rearrange the problem so the x does not appear next to the + sign. The result is $9 + 3x = 12$.

- Highlight the sign of operation so it is distinct from the variable. The result is 3x **+** 9 = 12.
- Read the equation out loud. Substitute "plus" for + and "equals" for =.
- Write the problem out, exaggerating the space between terms so it will look like this:

$$3x \quad + \quad 9 \quad = \quad 12$$

Place Value, Alignment, and Boxes

For younger students studying place value, 3-D boxes and index cards numbered 1 through 9 can help students grasp the right-to-left sequence of ones, tens, hundreds, and so on. For calculation, the boxes will have to be 2-D. By using large graph paper, students will be able to maintain the alignment of numbers with several places. This is particularly helpful for students with writing difficulties. Only one digit is allowed in each square on the graph paper. It may take some getting used to, but graph paper will be a valuable support for lengthy calculations, such as long division. If the student finds that the standard graph paper is not a good fit for her handwriting, the standard graph paper can be enlarged on a copier to allow adequate space for recording.

STRATEGIES THAT ADDRESS *VARIOUS DIFFICULTIES*

Strategies exist to address various difficulties, including verbal expression, anxiety, restlessness, time management, test preparation, and word retrieval.

The One That Got Away

Word Retrieval, Working Memory, Anxiety

She's got a fishing pole in the water. There's a tug. She landed one. She pulled it up. But somehow it escaped and returned to the water. Students who have problems with working memory often experience this frustration. They hear a question, "land" an answer, and raise their hand to share, but the response has disappeared into the recesses of their minds.

Tips for students who experience these problems:

- Guide them to jot down their thoughts. A short note is better than a short memory. "Splashdown" (see Chapter 9) works well.
- Help them develop something to say when this happens. Responses like "Can you come back to me?" or "I need another minute to

think" work well and help students save face in front of their peers. Encourage students to practice these lines at home.

- Tell them in advance which questions to anticipate. For example, tell them that they may be called on for questions that are multiples of eight.
- Establish a special cue that signals readiness. For example, tell them to raise their hand high in the air when they are prepared to respond.
- Provide a multiple-choice question instead of a fill-in-the blank one by asking, "Do you think that would be _____ or _____?"

Dumbo Had a Good Thing

Anxiety, Test Taking, Focus

I give students a small piece of green construction paper to use when taking tests. Students place it on the test sheet and move it down gradually as they progress. This helps in several ways by

- Enhancing focus by blocking extraneous stimuli.
- Forcing students to literally be in touch with the page.
- Giving them a comfort item, something to literally hang onto.

Cueing for Contribution

Verbal Expression, Word Retrieval

Responding to questions in class can be difficult for a student who experiences problems with

- Attention,
- Word retrieval,
- Processing speed,
- Memory, and/or
- Speaking before a group.

The following strategy can provide the student with more wait time and a greater chance for comfort and success. Prior to asking a question, prompt the student by saying,

"**I want you to think about** how Berlin's involvement in the Cold War was significant. **I'll come back to you in a few minutes, or you can raise your hand when you're ready to share.**"

The words in bold are the key features.

Tone of Voice

Anxiety

"Don't you talk to me in that tone, young man!" Have you heard or said that before? Often, the manner in which a message is conveyed is as important as the message itself. Wander the halls of the school and listen to faculty members with their very different vocal qualities. Listen to a book on CD and notice how the narrator's vocal quality affects comprehension and sustains attention.

Some students are extremely sensitive to vocal quality. Anxious students can be significantly affected by vocal quality. Vocal quality is not easy to alter, but it's important to recognize its effect on listeners, such as students.

If a student seems anxious, making a conscious effort to adjust vocal quality can result in increased comfort and an improved response. Consider the different tones that convey urgency, seriousness, warmth, and humor. What vocal quality will be the most soothing and reassuring?

Big Schedule, Big Clock

Time Management, Independent Functioning

This strategy can build independent functioning and improve time management skills. If the schedule is far from the clock, working memory comes into play. Students must look at the schedule and then hold that number in mind as they make their way to the clock. A watch is easier. On their way to the clock, students might get distracted and forget what they were doing and have to start all over. Sometimes, just knowing the location of the clock makes a difference in elapsed time when coordinating schedule and time. I have observed students who looked at the schedule three or four times to successfully match this information up "long distance" with the clock face. This trouble can be limited by placing schedules next to the clock. Both clock and schedule must be large enough for students to see them from any place in the room.

When questions arise, such as "When does this period end?" or "How many more minutes . . ." the response can simply be, "Look at the clock. I know you can figure it out."

If it's impossible to place a large clock and schedule together, setting a timer at the beginning of a class will work well also. Set it and forget it. Refer to "Ding!" in Chapter 7 on organization.

Tilt!

Visual-Motor Integration Skills, Copying

It's no surprise that students with dyslexia feel uncomfortable reading. Today, I watched a dyslexic young man use his cloth-bound binder as a book support for a loose sheet from which he was reading. I rotated his binder to give him a better incline. He grabbed the edges of the binder and actually got close to the material. He looked much more comfortable than if the sheet had been resting on a flat and slippery desk surface. I'm a fan of cloth binders, a bit of upholstery in an otherwise plastic school environment.

Bookstands can be very helpful as well. When a student is copying material from a book, placing the book on a bookstand facilitates the copying and creates more workspace on the desktop. It is easier to view items in a near-vertical position than a horizontal position. Lap desks tilted to facilitate reading are valuable for students who need time away from the desk. If many problems need to be copied, place a sticky note below the problem and move it along as needed. This helps a student keep his place on the page and speeds copying. It's easy to keep a stack of 10 to 20 notes inside the front of a text (especially math) for use on this type of task.

Quiet Fidgets

Restlessness and/or Anxiety

I had two test takers in my room and a third student whose fingers were dancing on the desktop as he pondered great thoughts. I quietly walked by and handed the fidgeter a small Koosh ball and whispered, "Here's a quiet fidget for you." The test takers actually thanked me, and the fidgeter, squishing the new object, went on unfazed.

For students whose hands are often in motion, hand exercisers, Koosh balls, beanbags, and other small, soft items give soothing, tactile feedback. These items don't make any noise—hence, the name "quiet fidgets."

All and Nothing

Test Preparation

Students come to me with one sheet completely filled in and ask, "Can you help me study this?" Many times, the requirement is memorization of information. It might be the keyboard on a word processor, or a map. Regardless, a completed sheet can't provide the opportunity to take a pretest or practice "filling in" the blanks.

I take the completed sheet and photocopy it. Then, I work with students to white out the information they will be required to recall. Finally, I photocopy that sheet for fill-in-type practice. This can be time consuming. It would be great to have two sheets from which to study: One would have all the information on it, and one would have none of the detailed information on it.

Color Me Organized

Tracking Papers

Sorting is a snap when things are color-coded. What if each department (English, math, science, etc.) used one color paper exclusively? This would make organization a breeze. Lined paper comes in colors or can be photocopied on colored paper. Graph paper, plain or colored, is fairly easy to sort. This strategy would help the most disorganized student retrieve wayward papers.

Also, it would add spice to moments at the copier. If teachers leave originals, fail to switch out colored paper in the trays, or leave the machine jammed, it would be easy to track down the perpetrator. Busted!

Columns for Comparison

Writing, Test Preparation, Note Taking

A teacher skillfully integrated the use of a graphic organizer into a lesson. She had students compare and contrast two viewpoints using two columns. The students had an opportunity to probe literature. In addition, they were taught a terrific brainstorming structure for comparison—columns. This is not necessarily a novel concept, but it works very well in many subjects and deserves reinforcement.

Do the students have ideas to compare or contrast?
   1. Draw vertical line(s).
   2. Use columns to sort differences and similarities.
   3. Now compare items point by point in writing or discussion.

Encourage students to use this technique on their tests and quizzes. Even if writing is not their strength, the columns will help them sort ideas and provide structure to their written responses.

Getting in the Game

Social/Performance Anxiety

Student participation in class is an integral part of learning and assessment. It appears on report cards and in comments. If a student is not participating, I try to figure out the cause before I make suggestions.

1. Some students lack sufficient knowledge to participate. They want to contribute, but they don't want to embarrass themselves. Once their skills improve, participation will as well. It's hard for these students to raise their hand because they may not know how to formulate a question. One-on-one instruction might work better for a while with these students until the knowledge gap is closed. For foreign-language classes, standard questions could be placed around the room or on the desk, to provide ready prompts for students.

2. Some students have a distinct learning style. Depending on the class, participation may vary greatly for these children. For example, strong visual learners might participate wholeheartedly in visual arts or computers, but in foreign language, their participation might be listening rather than speaking.

3. Some students have the knowledge but do not want to participate. These students may be uncomfortable in group situations. Perhaps they relate well one-on-one. They may be more introspective than their peers. Many of these students tote a book around (even at lunch) and are fueled by ideas shared on a page. Some of them are keen observers and listeners, and they just remain at a distance. Some are most comfortable with a sketchbook at hand.

If a teacher feels that lack of participation is affecting learning, some gentle nudging might be in order. The teacher could try the following:

> Explain that you would like to help the student increase his participation. Tell the student he needs to raise his hand at least once per class, even just to have something repeated or ask a question. If necessary, coach the student to ask, "Can you repeat that, please?" After a month, if all is going well, up the ante to two contributions per class. If the student is struggling with one oral participation, ask for a written contribution. Have him jot a comment or question. Hopefully, you can encourage and expand the child's comfort zone. I think of it as just getting in the game.

Too Much of a Good Thing

Impulsivity—Anxiety

Teachers encourage students to participate in class. Students' effort grade often reflects this aspect of their performance. Unlike reticent students described in "Getting in the Game" above, some students participate too much. They use a lot of air time. They may be ignorant of the give and take of class dynamics or seek a lot of reassurance. Many of these students are highly intelligent and have interesting comments to share.

Suggestions:

• Reinforce the value of comments.

• In private, guide such a student to see that the number of comments affects the class as a whole, given the time limitations and the number of students in class.

• Have him record the comments he would like to share and rank them himself according to the following system:

1 denotes extremely important and relevant.

2 denotes somewhat important and relevant.

3 denotes interesting but not relevant—this is a tangent.

• Tell him that during class only 1s will be accepted. Explain to him that 2s can be offered at another time. The goal is to get him to prioritize, select, and delay responses as needed.

Catching Up

Time Management for Students Who Have Been Absent

Being out of school for any reason can make a student feel uncomfortable. In the upper grades, several days out of school can be absolutely daunting. In certain circumstances, students are aware of times when they will miss school. They need to have a plan to get back in the game. I put together a stepwise worksheet to give students a tangible way to approach teachers and help them organize the multilevel task of catching up.

Catching Up—Before or After Absences

Teacher/Subject: _____

Materials:

What books do I need? _____

Pack them.

What worksheets do I need? _____

Get worksheets and pack them.

Assignments:

What are the assignments? _____

Record in assignment book.

Are there any tests I need to make up? _____

Is there a review sheet for that test? Yes____ No___

If yes, get review sheet.

What day, date, and time should I take the test? _____

Where should I take it? _____

Record date and place in assignment book.

Are there any quizzes I need to make up? _____

What material will be covered on the quiz? _____

Pack needed materials.

What day, date, and time should I take the quiz? _____

Where should I take it? _____

Mark assignment book.

Can I get notes for the days I missed?

Could I ask someone to take Penned Notes?

Ask them.

Collect Penned Notes forms from the office/learning specialist.

Give Penned Notes to your note taker.

Will the notes be available elsewhere (computer programs)?_____

Is there a presentation I could review?_____

Is there anything else I can do to catch up? _____

"Thank you very much for helping me catch up. I really appreciate your time."

Color Me Comprehensible

Map Comprehension

In a geography class, students began to study a map by coloring the bodies of water and countries with colored pencils. The students relaxed and enjoyed this nonverbal task. The coloring revealed important information:

- Proportion of water to land
- Distinction between peninsulas and islands

Colors showed a clearer visual representation. In fact, the students were able to distinguish a landform whose outline is very similar to that of a body of water. I wonder if this would have been possible without the coloring practice. In addition to providing an opportunity for relaxation and a clearer representation of information, coloring often enhances memory through tactile feedback.

Here's one for *Jeopardy*:

Answer: This body of water in North America is very similar in shape to the Florida peninsula.

Question: What is Hudson Bay?

Materials Modification

Materials modification has more to do with the *how* of learning than the *what*. Materials can be modified without changing the curriculum or adjusting the program.

For example, visually complex maps may pose a challenge to students who have difficulty perceiving visual details. Maps can be modified by deleting extraneous details. For example, lines of latitude and longitude can be deleted, assuming they're not related to instructional objectives. By deleting extraneous visual details, the features on the map become more prominent. Another simple modification is enlargement of materials.

Caveat: If significant modifications are needed, it's probably time to look at obtaining different materials.

Quantifying Clueless

Test Preparation

For test preparation, guide students to prioritize units of information (vocabulary, identifications, formulas, etc.) by rating them 1, 2, or 3. Students should skim through material on the study guide, the worksheet, or past assessments and jot numbers in the left-hand margin to indicate how well they know the information.

1 denotes "I know this—I'm certain."

2 denotes "I'm not sure—I sort of know."

3 denotes "I have no idea—I'm clueless."

Once information is rated, students will no longer start studying at the top of a paper and work their way down. They start on 3s, move on to 2s, and review 1s if time allows.

When I say, "Tell me some of your 3s," many more hands go up than if I ask, "Is there anyone here who is stymied by a word?"

Students are more comfortable acknowledging a 3 than saying they do not know. It is as if the information is being rated rather than the student.

I call this technique 1–2–3 prioritization.

SUMMARY

Strategies are the meat and potatoes of support services. These tips are designed to improve many different skills, including memory, writing, reading, memorization, note taking, restlessness, sustained attention, time management, math, test taking, test preparation, and map interpretation. Many of these techniques apply to topics across the curriculum and to students across grade levels.

By observing students carefully, analyzing the task at hand, and noting error patterns, the need for specific strategies becomes evident. For example, many beginning writers confuse *topic sentence* with *thesis statement*, which can result in many different errors. The solution: Require students to put their thesis statements in bold. With this done, students can easily refer to their thesis statement and note if subsequent points support it. Over time, students tend to visualize the placement and purpose of this bold thesis statement.

Strategies can increase interest, as well as skill. For example, the name and format of the technique "Beat It!" often appeals to students with a competitive nature. Also, when used as feedback for students, emphasizing numbers as opposed to words may appeal to students who are more mathematically inclined. For example, "This looks like a 3. Supply more details and enhance vocabulary to bring it to a 7."

The names of strategies may support the teaching. For younger students, the "Flying Apostrophe" will help students visualize the position above the line. When teachers consistently refer to techniques by the same name, students are likely to develop an internal prompt of their own, as in "Touch the Page" and "Pick It! Stick It!"

Finally, by using names, teachers can ask students to use various strategies for assignments. For example, after demonstrating "Envelope Sort," (see Chapter 6) a social studies teacher might give homework, such as "Read pages 40–45. Develop an envelope sort for all highlighted names."

7 Organization

Techniques to Get It Together

Students who are organized have many advantages over those who are not: They have completed assignments, prepared for tests, and stored materials in designated places; they have adequate supplies; and they can locate supplies, materials, and assignments readily. Picture the confidence that such students possess when approaching a classroom. They are ready—and they know it. Now, contrast this image with that of students who struggle with organization. They did not complete the assignment, or perhaps they did but left it at home. Perhaps they completed the homework and brought it to school, but they cannot locate it in their binder. They dash to class and realize instantly that they don't have a pencil, the text, or perhaps a calculator. They don't have the tools to go forward in class. Imagine how these students feel. Many days at school, they will arrive tardy to class while apologizing or explaining "unprepared" scenarios, requesting a pencil or book, or asking for an extension, all in front of their peers.

Disorganization can seem like a plague. Gifted students experiencing this difficulty are often dubbed "the absent-minded professor." This expression may fit the picture but minimizes the disadvantage organizational difficulties present in a school setting. I have seen students who were more than capable of producing top-flight work. If they could not submit it on time, however, the consequences were daunting. The efforts on an A+ research paper might actually earn a D if the paper takes 3 days to locate.

The relatively new term *executive functioning* describes a set of organizational skills necessary in life. The main skills include setting a goal, making a plan, recognizing priorities, initiating a response to high-priority tasks, sustaining on-task efforts while delaying or blocking response to low-priority tasks, flexibly switching from one task to another, and completing high-priority tasks. Students with executive dysfunction struggle to anticipate or allocate the time needed for their school work. They need techniques to help them break a significant project into manageable units of work. In addition, they need help designating "chunks" within the project, recording due dates for each "chunk," and sticking to the work plan.

The skill of preparation has many components. One key component is allocating time to complete each task; however, some students are so active after school that they simply do not have adequate time to prepare and carry out an action plan.

Parents can help their children with organization in many ways. They can provide much-needed guidance in establishing a balanced schedule for their child. For students with executive dysfunction, allowing plenty of time for ongoing planning and organization is critical. In addition, parents can provide necessary school supplies for their children. I encourage parents to buy "backup" supplies if their child is disorganized. Things get lost, and the relief of knowing an extra protractor is available is worth far more than the cost of the item itself. Finally, parents can help and support their child in allocating and reserving a portion of the home for the transitions to and from school.

DO THE COMBO MAMBO

Working a round, dial-type combination lock is difficult. Students need to remember many specifics:

1. Three numbers (often several digits) for their lock

2. The correct sequence of the numbers

3. When to spin past zero

4. Which rotation to use for each number (clockwise or counterclockwise)

5. Knowing what the above terms mean

6. To pause briefly once each number is aligned

Working memory, focus, and eye-hand coordination all come into play in an often noisy environment during a frequently transitional and limited time. This task can be intimidating for many students. One simple support is to put very tiny dots on the numbers needed. Dark-colored nail polish works well and should be removed as soon as the student has mastered the technique. The dots are not evident except on close inspection.

Naturally, for security reasons, the "dotting" should be done at a time when other students cannot observe.

PARKAS IN JULY

No one wants to shop for school supplies early. It's like taking off a baseball cap to try on a woolen hat. Still, such tools of the trade as binders, dividers, book covers, and pencils are crucial to student success. The right kind and number can make an enormous difference. The time to shop is when stores are well stocked but crowds have not yet arrived. Go in late July. Not only will choices be plenty, but the experience will be pleasant. If you are uncertain as to the needed supplies, contact the school. Mark the calendar now. Just do it!

THINKING AHEAD AND PLANNING BACKWARD

Record the due date on the calendar. The paper is due the **28th**. Now work backward. Prior to turning the final copy in, changes need to be made to the rough draft, and the paper needs to be saved and printed (two copies due to Murphy's Law). This could take 2 days, so allowing for Murphy's Law again (the ink cartridge could be dry), figure 3 days, which brings this chunk of the task to the **25th**.

The previous chunk involves the teacher looking at the rough draft to provide feedback to the student. This will take a week. Teachers also are subject to Murphy's Law, so we'll allow 8 days, which brings the due date for the rough draft to the **17th**.

Putting together a rough draft can take a good deal of time, depending on the length and type of the paper. Assuming this is not an extensive research paper, I would allow 4 days for development of the rough draft (introduction, body paragraphs, conclusion), so Murphy's Law brings it to 5 days, or the **12th**.

Prior to beginning the rough draft, it is critical to review the assignment as it was given. In addition, a review of recent class notes and reflection is needed. Sometimes, a student will want to contact classmates as well. I will call this part of the process "pondering." It is not an involved chunk, so I will assign 1 day, and Murphy's Law makes that 2, so pondering begins on the **10th**. Obviously, if a student wants feedback earlier or in several steps, the timeline could be adjusted.

10th: Begin pondering

12th: Begin writing rough draft

17th: Submit rough draft to teacher

25th: Make changes to rough draft, save on computer, print two copies

28th: Turn in final paper

DISABILITY VERSUS DISINTEREST

Organizational difficulties exist and are often referred to as "executive dysfunction." The attending problems include difficulty planning time, space, and materials. Executive dysfunction often coexists with ADHD.

Disinterest in organization is quite common, particularly in adolescents who have many other interests competing for their time. Some people don't want to be organized at any age. They are more "go with the flow," spontaneous types who tend to view planning as restrictive.

If a student has disability and interest, certain systems can be taught and specific checkpoints established. If a student has both disability and disinterest, it's unlikely that he will be able to make a substantial change in organizational practices on his own, and it will be important to get someone else to do the organizing. Having parents provide this support can be tricky. Organizational coaches are the best answer; however, the student will need to agree with the systems established by the organizational coach. For this reason, many organizational coaches try to strike a compromise between the student's needs and wants. In his adult life, the person with disability and disinterest in organization is likely to need a top-notch assistant.

PRACTICAL ASSIGNMENT FOR SEPTEMBER

In the first week of school, here is an assignment designed to support organization:

- Using Comic Sans font, size 14, type two packing lists. One will be entitled *For School*. The other will be entitled **For Home**.
- List the materials needed for each class in the order they appear on the schedule (e.g., first period, second period, and so on).
- Abbreviate **a**ssignment book as A and **b**inder as B.
- Use color and space to differentiate morning and afternoon classes. Use a special sign, such as *, to indicate a class that is part of a rotation on the schedule.
- Post *For School* at the home-packing location, otherwise known as the launching and landing pad.
- Post **For Home** inside the locker or book bag.

ORGANIZING ORGANIZATION

Begin by asking questions and observing behavior to determine where the problem originates. Is this a problem at home or at school?

The following analysis lists the *At School* tasks in italics and the **At Home** tasks in bold.

Each organizational task is analyzed separately. "Possible Problems" and "Possible Solutions" are recorded for each task. The problems and solutions are visually coded to help the school and family identify and respond to organizational issues.

This analysis may look complex, but many teachers and families have told me it has been a valuable tool.

Analysis of Organizational Problems

I. Task: Getting Assignments in the First Place

  A. Possible Problems

    1. *Student doesn't record homework correctly and completely due to problems with attention, copying, handwriting, or pace.*

    2. *Assignment book is lost.*

    3. **Student tries to get homework off computer, but there are computer problems.**

  B. Possible Solutions

    1. *Teachers give assignments at beginning of class.*

    2. *Teachers give more time to record assignments.*

    3. *Teachers initial assignment book at end of class.*

    4. *Student gets another assignment book (if available at school).*

    5. **Student asks family to get new assignment book.**

    6. **Parents obtain a new assignment book.**

    7. **Adults contact technology coordinator to resolve computer problems.**

    8. **Student contacts peer by phone to obtain assignment.**

II. Tasks: Doing, Packing, and Bringing Assignments to School

  A. Possible Problems

    1. *Student didn't bring home right materials to complete work.*

    2. **Student doesn't check assignment book and/or computer, depending on how assignments are recorded.**

   3. **Student does not have enough time to complete assignments due to too many extracurricular activities.**

   4. **Student has trouble waking up, has not packed, rushes to catch bus, and forgets important materials.**

B. Possible Solutions

   1. *Student makes a packing list and tapes it inside his locker.*

   2. *Teachers dismiss students 2 minutes earlier to ensure careful packing.*

   3. *Student centralizes all assignments in one place—the assignment book. Assignments posted on the board and/or the computer are recorded in assignment book.*

   4. **Family decides to reduce the number of after-school activities.**

   5. **Student packs for school at night rather than in the morning.**

   6. **Family and student set alarms to consider slow starts.**

   7. **Student posts packing list near the place where backpack is stored (launching and landing pad).**

   8. **Parents purchase copies of school texts to keep at home.**

III. Task: Turning In Assignments at School

A. Possible Problems

   1. *The binder, backpack, and/or locker are full of papers stored in random order.*

   2. *The student cannot locate the assignment she says she did.*

   3. **The binder and/or backpack are broken.**

B. Possible Solutions

   1. *Student weeds out binder at school (see "1–2–3 Weed Out!" below).*

   2. *Student cleans out and organizes locker. A peer can assist.*

   3. *Teachers provide regular time for weeding out binder, backpack, and locker.*

   4. **Parents remind student to weed out papers once a week as a routine.**

   5. **Student weeds out binder at home (see "1–2–3 Weed Out!" below).**

   6. **Parents purchase appropriate materials to support organization (the best-quality binders have rings aligned and plastic slant-cut dividers. The best-quality spirals have two double coils).**

IV. Task: Getting Assignments Signed

    A. Possible Problems

        1. **Student can't find papers to be signed.**

        2. **Student forgets to ask parents for signature.**

    B. Possible Solutions

        1. *Student designates a section of binder for all forms, letters, and tests that need to be shared with parents, and marks it as "home" section.*

        2. **Parents ask nightly, "Do you have any papers I need to see or sign for school?"**

        3. **Student sets watch or beeper to go off every night at the same time to remind her to ask for parent signature.**

WHY WOMEN CAN'T BORROW PURSES

Each woman has her own system that has taken years to perfect. She could find a lipstick or Sam's Club card with her eyes closed. Each has her own stuff. ChapStick requires a zippered compartment, and prescription sunglasses need an inside pouch. Some purses even have interior lights for the woman who drives a lot at night.

Most organizational systems are developed through trial and error. Many purses are returned or donated. What works for one will not necessarily work for another. How does this relate to students?

I doubt any one system will work for students of different ages, needs, and temperaments. Establishing an organizational system that is entirely uniform does not tend to work well for a mix of students. There is a need to customize storage solutions and organizational systems for individuals. Here are some suggestions to help with this task:

- Find out *how* a student wants to store his stuff.
- Make sure he can tell you *why* he wants to store it that way.
- Discuss the systems he has tried. What was successful? What did not work, and why not? Let him try the new system for a week. Then meet to discuss the outcome.

There's an enormous selection of choices. Consider the following:

- Accordion files
- Two binders for storing morning and afternoon class materials

- One mega binder
- Multiple binders—one for each subject

PREPARING FOR TEACHER TUTORING

Some students may dutifully show up for tutoring but have no idea how to use the time. Some students need a prompt. Others might need a script. Here are some questions and tips you can offer. Teachers and advisors can give the tips below to students who can simply refer to them before they go for a teacher's help.

- Bring paper and pencil.
- Do I want help with a test that I took?

  Bring the test.

- Which type of question or problem gave me the most trouble?

  Highlight or underline this area on the test.

- Do I want help to prepare for a future test?

  Ask about the format: Will it include short answers, essays, definitions, and identifications? Will I be able to use notes or formulas? Jot down what your teacher says.

- Is there a particular topic that confuses me?

  Bring examples of difficult exercises and homework.

- Is there a CD, practice sheet, or Web site I can visit to review material?

  Jot this information down.

BINDER BLUES

Students don't put papers in their binder for several reasons:

1. Some are slow to pack up, often due to processing-speed issues or difficulty with transitions. They don't have time between classes to file loose sheets. They race to the next class and just stuff papers in the front pocket of the binder, saying to themselves, "I'll straighten these out later."

2. Some can't open and close the rings due to fine motor problems. These students often have very poor handwriting.

3. Binders have misaligned rings. This is particularly common after several months of school.

The following system seems to help many students:

1. Get transparent plastic dividers that are "slant cut" and three-hole punched.

2. Get multiple packages of these dividers. Students may need two to five dividers of each color for different designations, such as "tests and quizzes," "notes," and so forth.

3. Designate a color for each subject. English is blue, science is green, and so forth.

4. Label each divider with a permanent marker. English grammar, English tests and quizzes, and English vocabulary, for example, could all be blue dividers.

Students can now file papers by sliding them into the proper divider—no more fighting with rings!

BACK TO BASICS

Here are A-B-C-D categories to help students organize key materials and storage areas.

Assignment Book

Paper clip current page with previous ones for rapid flip.

Fill in all boxes (subjects and dates). Write the word *none* or the number 0 if nothing is assigned.

Write "Look ahead" or draw an arrow toward the date if a test or project is beyond the week's glance.

Highlight special events and assignments.

Mark parent signature (for test and quizzes) with *P* in box.

Mark completed assignments by drawing an *X* through them.

Tear out unnecessary pages, such as those that are 1 month old or more.

*B*inder

Put reinforcements on papers that need them.

Weed out old papers.

Inventory loose-leaf paper.

Clean Out Book Bag

Bring trash receptacle and recycling bin nearby.

Remove all loose pieces of paper.

Lighten your load.

De-clutter Locker

Bring trash receptacle and recycling bin nearby.

1–2–3 WEED OUT!

There are three basic categories of stuff:

1. Need now (binder or folders)

2. Save for later (files at home or locker)

3. Discard (trash or recycle)

I suggest that students perform 1–2–3 Weed Out in a specific location. Using the same place each time will reinforce and speed the process. Students will need a large surface and a trash receptacle and recycling bin nearby.

The trickiest category is the second one. Students should check with teachers to be sure that information can be removed from the binder.

Just two piles and 15 minutes can help bring order to chaos and restore the student's sense of control over materials.

SCHEDULE FOR TEACHER HELP

This simple schedule can help clarify student responsibilities. Many students need visual reinforcement to keep them on track. This schedule seems to work well for students who are forgetful, avoidant, or both.

If the teacher help time occurs during "free" time, I suggest giving students at least one day a week "free." Teachers can write "FREE" across that day. If a student needs teacher tutoring more than twice a week, the parents and the learning specialist should be aware of this arrangement.

Teacher-Help Schedule for _____				
Monday	*Tuesday*	*Wednesday*	*Thursday*	*Friday*
Teacher	Teacher	Teacher	Teacher	Teacher
Room	Room	Room	Room	Room
Time	Time	Time	Time	Time

REAL ESTATE AGENTS ARE RIGHT

Real estate agents are right: location, location, and location. Pencil sharpeners go next to pencils. Stamps go next to envelopes. The key is to locate a book, paper, or supply near the place of its use. Pair function with location. Follow this simple rule, and life will be simpler, more efficient, and less frustrating.

BORDERING ON MADNESS

Certain events and times of year bring stress, as well as excitement. To manage the stress and maximize the enjoyment, mark off two weeks on either side of holidays, exams, special celebrations, trips, drama presentations, tournaments, and so forth. Do not plan *anything* extra during these two weeks. No exceptions can be made. Use every day fully, and refuse or postpone any additional responsibilities. Allowing "spillage" time for the stress and excitement of special times will preserve everyone's sanity and allow the times to be naturally special.

LAUNCHING AND LANDING PAD

The idea behind this strategy is to centralize all school-related items that go back and forth to school on a regular basis. I suggest students speak with their parents to select a spot near the entrance or exit of their home. Once the space is agreed upon, a suitable container, such as a large box, a basket, a plastic tub, an empty drawer, or anything that will work for both the parent and the student, can be obtained. I encourage the student to decorate his container. This is fun, establishes a positive association, taps into artistic intelligence, and can work as an attention-getting device. Next, I ask the student to name the container, even something simple, such as "Alice's School Box." Students may use their verbal intelligence to craft something a bit more sophisticated. All school-related items go in the box. Reminders, such as "doughnuts for Monday group" or "special dress for trip," can go in the container or be taped to the outside. When homework is complete, binder, books, and supplies all go in the box. The backpack sits next to the box. It needs to be emptied every afternoon and repacked every evening. Morning packing is a major no-no since this is such a crunch time for many households.

Without centralization, materials end up by the phone, on the kitchen table, inside the desk drawer, next to the computer, or by the TV. The creation of the launching and landing pad marks the end of materials being scattered throughout the home. Until centralizing is second nature to the student, all alternate locations should be checked nightly, and any stray materials should be promptly corralled in the student's school container.

STUDENT INFORMATION AND RESOURCES

Students need to centralize key information. This form should be completed in early September and placed in the binder. A copy should also be made for home.

Personal Directory

In case of illness, absence, or emergency:
Family phone
At home _____Work _____ Cell _____
School main number _____
Advisor name _____ Phone _____ E-mail _____

Student Support

In each subject, name two classmates who could help you if needed:

Subject _____
Student _____Phone _____E-mail_____
Student _____ Phone _____ E-mail _____

Subject _____

Student _____ Phone _____ E-mail _____

Student _____ Phone _____ E-mail _____

Subject _____

Student _____ Phone _____ E-mail _____

Student _____ Phone _____ E-mail _____

TRACKING TEACHERS

Encourage students to jot specific days, times, and places when teachers are available to help. Advise students to confirm the meeting times and to record them in their planners. Remind students to bring materials and questions to teachers for help.

Teacher _____ E-mail _____

Days and times _____

Teacher _____ E-mail _____

Days and times _____

Teacher _____ E-mail _____

Days and times _____

Teacher _____ E-mail _____

Days and times _____   _____

REMINDERS THAT WORK

Little slips of paper are often used to record reminders. Most of them end up crumpled at the bottom of a tote, book bag, or handbag. They get lost, ripped, and mashed. Often, they get discarded. They aren't durable or attention getting. Ironically, they are forgettable reminders.

The best kind of reminder would be made of florescent steel that beeps. My compromise is to use neon-colored index cards. Color can symbolize meaning. For example, jot school reminders on orange cards and home reminders on blue cards.

In years past, all index cards were white, as were file folders and paper. Let's add a little life and interest to the task of learning. Color it memorable.

LONG-RANGE PLANNING

Many students record the due date for long-range assignments and/or tests. If this is all they write down, they may not take action until their note comes into view. By then, it's usually too late for adequate preparation time. The key is to make sure students record the LRP (long-range project) each day as an assignment. By recording the assignment daily, students will have a visual tickler. Recording the number of days left until the final due date will be even more valuable. An assignment book entry might appear as follows:

2/7/07

LRP 14 days until final draft.

Many adolescents use two categories of time for planning purposes:

1. Now

2. Not now

Using LRP will create a bridge between these categories.

TAKE CONTROL

Teachers control what is assigned and when it is due. Students must record, look at, complete, pack, and submit the assignment. I want to encourage teachers to exercise their control.

The very best time to review upcoming assignments, clarify expectations, and record appropriate details is at the *beginning* of class. This is not always easy to do, but it will make a big difference for students who have trouble with assignments.

At the end of class, distractions are greater, and students are tired and ready to move on to the next class.

Teachers can model organization for their students by giving assignments every day as part of a routine.

PROMOTING TOTING

The action of opening a suitcase is the beginning of a series of very *intentional* behaviors. Some people make a list of items to take on a trip. Others keep a copy of this list in the suitcase itself. Others keep a travel kit filled with personal items "at the ready."

Placing items in a tote, bag, or case encourages conscious choices. This process is not nearly as intentional for someone simply gathering items to carry in his arms. Encourage students to pack a bag to carry needed materials. They will think about what needs to go in the bag for classes, and at the end of a class, they can simply toss materials into the bag and head off to their next class. Sturdy canvas totes are open at the top so the contents are clearly visible. They can stand alone without flopping over and are readily accessible—no zippers, Velcro, or drawstrings.

Pack a bag and go!

PUTTING TANGENTS IN THEIR PLACE

Tangential thinking is a regular occurrence for

- Creative thinkers (one idea leads to another),
- Multitaskers (operate on several levels simultaneously),
- Persons with ADHD, and/or
- Persons with executive dysfunction.

A thought comes to mind, but it may not be the time or place to talk about or take action on it. Still, a student feels she does not want to lose track of the thought. What can she do?

Make a special place for tangents called the Tangent Locker. Corners make good places for Tangent Lockers. I use the upper right-hand corner of a sheet of paper to record my tangential thoughts. I draw a line so the corner of the sheet forms a triangle and record my tangents in the triangle.

Tangents are usually interesting and important—just not timely. Check Tangent Lockers regularly.

DISTINCTIVE GEAR

Luggage carousels are filled with suitcases, most of which are black and hard to tell apart. The same is true for book bags and books. Encourage students to take a little time to add something to their gear that will distinguish it from others'. Monograms can be helpful. Colorful tape, tags, or ribbon can help too. Names must be on or in all materials. This is absolutely essential.

SPARE BINDER IN THE CLASSROOM

Particularly in the beginning of school, students with executive dysfunction may arrive without adequate supplies or materials. This is a fairly tricky situation since most students cannot drive to obtain their materials or supplies. The scenario often plays out in the following way:

The student is reminded several times but continues to show up without the necessary materials. After the first week or 10 days, the teacher communicates with the parent. The parent often says he did not receive a supply list and is irritated that action was not taken sooner.

Why not have a "spare" binder in the classroom? Initially, it could be used to model a system for organizing papers. If needed, it could then be given to a student.

EXTRA! EXTRA!

When students misplace or lose materials between home and school, it is wise to obtain duplicate copies of texts. One stays at home, and the other stays at school. This lightens the students' load mentally and physically.

Pencils are easily lost, but teachers do not have an infinite supply to hand out to students. At the beginning of the year, a student with executive dysfunction could bring in 12 dozen pencils. He could then distribute a dozen or two to each teacher for his use as he informs the teacher about his organizational difficulties. When a student did this with me, I felt it was a very proactive step and was impressed with the student's initiative.

IN LIEU OF LOCKERS

Think of a noisy, crowded place. People move over, under, and around each other. Amid this relative chaos, an individual challenged by attention and/or organization is expected to perform a detail-sensitive task (locker combination), locate important materials, and gather them quickly.

This scene takes place not in a subway but in a locker room. As an alternative, inquire about setting aside a spot for student storage in the learning specialist's room. Perhaps an advisor would also be willing to provide some space. The key is that the special storage spot be located in a fairly central location.

Now think of a place without locks where materials remain safe. Imagine being able to ask for help. Finally, expect to receive reassurance and some cues for staying on track for the next class—all this in lieu of lockers.

ACCESSIBLE ASSIGNMENTS

A student may rush to pack up at the end of the day. Even if she has packing lists prepared and posted on her locker, she'll need to have current information at her fingertips. Often, the assignment book is stored inside a binder. Getting the information she needs will require several steps. To some students, the homework book seems buried within the cavernous interior of the mega binder. Time is precious, so she may not look but just grab materials and hope for the best. By the time she checks her assignment book, she may be home, at which point it will be too late if materials are missing.

Keeping the assignment book separate from the binder works well. It can be hooked to the pencil case by placing three circular metal loops through the three holes. Bingo—easy access to writing implement and homework book.

WHAT'S GOING ON?

When students continue to fall behind on assignments, it is valuable to know why. Often, students are unaware of how their time is spent. Having them record their activities for 1 week will increase their awareness and answer teacher questions. The following table can be adjusted to facilitate this assignment. This activity is not in any way intended to be punitive but is undertaken in a spirit of problem solving. In one case, the schedule revealed that a student spent a great deal of time traveling to and from activities in which his sibling was involved. The car needed to function as a work station for this student. As a result of the time analysis, the car was outfitted with a lap desk and necessary school supplies.

What's Going On? For one week, jot what you are doing after school. The times are approximate. I know you don't do everything in half-hour intervals.					
	Monday	Tuesday	Wednesday	Thursday	Friday
4:30					
5:00					
5:30					
6:00					
6:30					
7:00					
7:30					
8:00					
8:30					
9:00					
9:30					
10:00					

TOOLS OF THE TRADE

Most students cannot drive and purchase their own materials, so, parents, this is your moment to really support your budding scholar. For example, mechanical pencils with a fingertip advance button will work best for students who experience fine motor control difficulties. The size of the lead can make a difference too. If it's too thin, it will break often. If it's too thick, it will smudge. Highlighters that operate like a ballpoint pen will last longer than those with separate caps. Ask the learning specialist and teachers for suggestions.

DING!

Many students have difficulty planning their use of time, space, and materials. Students who demonstrate specific and significant troubles in these areas may be diagnosed with executive dysfunction. Increasing a student's awareness of time can help him complete assignments on time. Using a timer can increase interest and efficiency. Some digital timers beep before the time is "up." They beep when 10 minutes remain, when 5 minutes remain, and finally when the time has elapsed. They provide audible reminders to stay on task, pick up the pace, or ask for more time. If the student sets the timer, the time reminders then become results of his effort, which make them quite different from the verbal reminder of another person. There is no "nag" element. These timers are available at some of the larger kitchen and bath stores. They are inexpensive, can stand alone (with a fold-out easel on back), and often have a magnet. Keeping track of time on task can be simpler and more accurate with one of these terrific little gadgets.

SUMMARY

In the fall, getting students off on the right foot can help set the tone for the entire year. In this regard, parents have substantial influence. Obtaining the supplies and materials required by the school can boost a child's self-confidence as he enters a classroom, knowing he is prepared. Over the course of the year, items get lost. This certainly goes for adults, as well as children. Parents are encouraged to anticipate this fact of life and obtain additional pencils, notebook paper, index cards, and paper and ink for the computer. Thinking ahead will help reduce those dreaded last-minute runs to the store and even save money on gasoline.

Also, purchasing "distinctive gear" will help the student locate his backpack and binder with ease. Solicit the child's input about a timer, and bring him along to shop for one with features he wants. He will likely be more invested in using the timer to improve time management.

Teachers are not in a position to address organizational difficulties. Often, they teach study and time management skills; however, if students cannot or will not apply these skills throughout the day, teachers can do little. After school, parents can guide students to establish routines that will enhance organization. Establishing a launching and landing pad at home will help centralize materials.

Centralization works for planning as well. If home and school calendars are consolidated, everyone can see at a glance all that the day will require. As the section "Bordering on Madness" emphasized, the calendar should reflect the additional activities involved at holidays. Both academic and home requirements must be on the calendar. For example, a test might be scheduled for Friday. If the family plans for Thursday night are to attend a sporting event, the student will be in a crunch for time. Something's got to give. Either the student studies Wednesday night (clearly not optimal), or the family needs to forego the event.

Consistency and routines help students maintain order. For example, declaring Sunday nights for "1–2–3 Weed Out!" will keep binders organized in minimum time. Think of it as taking out the trash. Perhaps designate Weed Out and trash take-out on the same day.

This brings up the point of after-school activities. The amount of time required for participation needs to be given careful consideration. Before committing to a school play or a swim team, speak with the program director about the necessary time commitment.

Many students are extremely happy to sign up for various activities, but later, they feel conflicted about competing requirements. Parents need to take an active role in guiding their child to achieve a balance.

Students can increase their academic success by identifying resources and support. The information in "Tracking Teachers" is a valuable guide to accessing support. Encourage students to record this information at the beginning of every semester or trimester.

8 Test Format

Facilitating Accurate Assessment

Students will prepare for a test and may know all the information required. They may have fully mastered the content. Sometimes, however, they are not able to manage how their knowledge is assessed. Teachers may be masterful with students in the classroom, brilliant, and passionate about their subject matter; however, they may not be aware of what they are asking a student to do on a test, unrelated to the content.

It's all about task analysis. What is being asked of the student? What skills are involved? These skills are distinct from content mastery. For example, when students record answers directly on paper, the skill of handwriting features prominently in their response. For a student with writing difficulties, if there is a fill-in-the-blank response, the blank or line may pose an obstacle if it is not long enough. The student may end up compacting her response or writing it curled up along the side margin, which can be time consuming. Copying is an example of another skill unrelated to content. Tests often involve copying, and teachers assume students will not have trouble with this task. Unfortunately, some do have such trouble—math problems constitute the most common area of difficulty—and this can result in errors and longer-than-average response times. If students are challenged by a number of different test format issues, they likely will lag their peers in performance. They may become anxious as they become aware of their pace compared with that of those around them. Students often say they hear their classmates turning the pages before them.

The visual format of the test can have a strong effect on students with visual perceptual difficulties. In general, if a test is prepared on a word processor, copies are crisp, and the contrast is sharp. In this case, students with visual perceptual problems will fare well. A handwritten test, however, leaves the student at the mercy of the teacher's handwriting skills. Consider the handwriting of those you know. Few teachers have grown to adulthood without some compromise in their initially clear penmanship. It is not uncommon for students to ask a learning specialist to read the question simply because they cannot decipher the teacher's handwriting.

Small glitches may start to snowball for a student taking the test. Frequently, the final grade reflects the sum of challenges to the student. Assuming that the child prepared sufficiently for an assessment, the parents and child are bewildered at the outcome. If the scenario is repeated, self-esteem and test anxiety can become more prominent issues for the student.

HIT "ENTER" FOR MULTIPLE CHOICE

When typing a test, it's probably easier to enter multiple-choice answers all in one line, like this:

A) Gettysburg B) Bull Run C) Vicksburg D) Antietam

For a student with visual perceptual problems, the task can be complicated by visual scanning and discrimination skills. For longer responses, the challenge becomes even greater. For words that are hyphenated at the end of a line, the difference is significant.

It would be a huge help to students if teachers would hit the "Enter" key between choices, like this:

A) Gettysburg

B) Bull Run

C) Vicksburg

D) Antietam

Get the students to "show what they know" by eliminating possible obstacles in the assessment process, such as visual layout.

CREATIVE TESTS

As part of an assessment, a social studies teacher required students to use the tune to *The Brady Bunch* and rewrite the lyrics for it to include

15 detailed facts about life in the Depression, including presidents, New Deal, and Dust Bowl.

Crafting this type of assessment is not easy, but students respond very positively to it. Students who took this test actually enjoyed it. For students who often experience test anxiety, this "outside the box" type of test might be a good surprise.

WORD BANKS HIGH

I once noticed that a student kept lifting his arm while taking a test. He was glancing at the word bank located at the bottom of the page. The writing position for both righties and lefties will obscure material placed at the bottom of the page. The solution is simple: Place word banks at the top of the page.

A TEST THAT TAUGHT

A teacher came to ask my opinion of a history test where the main requirement was to write a persuasive essay.

To draw a parallel: English teachers expect that students will link "well-developed essay" with topic sentence, supporting detail, transitions, examples, quotations, concluding sentence, and thesis statement. Many English teachers will specify these elements on tests.

I imagine history teachers expect that students will link "key elements of an era/battle/period" with specific names, dates, events, places, outcomes, trends, and so forth. This history teacher provided a list of specifics in much the same way as an English teacher would, stating, "A good essay would contain clear uses of some of the following words . . ." An analysis and sequence of the words provided in this way would enable students to write better essays. This technique is particularly valuable for students with word retrieval difficulties, test anxiety, and memory issues.

In addition, the teacher provided a photograph pertinent to the essay at the bottom of the page. This stimulus is likely to appeal to nonverbal learners and may act as a more effective prompt than words.

TESTING ACCOMMODATIONS FOR ALL

The following suggestions are designed to minimize stress and emphasize content mastery:

Relax Format Requirements

Do not require complete sentences. This might not work for English, but teachers of other subjects could just ask students to respond by jotting phrases that include the key terms and concepts.

Permit standard abbreviations, such as w/, b/c, dept., Pres., Am., and so forth.

Permit symbols, such as & and +.

These accommodations will help students to

Finish within the allotted time,

Put the focus squarely on subject mastery,

Have enough time to check their answers, and

Write less. (With back-to-back tests, hand fatigue is a real issue.)

Offer Chewy Candy During the Test

- This provides sensory feedback, which can help manage stress. Put the trash can in front of the door so students cannot leave with a mouthful of candy.

Eliminate Extra Credit Questions

- In my experience, these questions are usually valuable for strong students. Students with learning difficulties often feel pressured to attempt them. The students who benefit are those with the least need to do so.

COLOR-CODED TESTS

A math teacher developed a clever and creative test format to clarify the three distinct parts of her test:

- The first part was timed with no calculator permitted.
- The second part was untimed with no calculator permitted.
- The third part was untimed with a calculator permitted.

It was simple to administer, and the distinctions were clear to students because the teacher had written the problems on three different-colored papers—one for each part of the test.

MEET THEM HALFWAY

The majority of students with learning disabilities have difficulty with printed material. They may struggle with reading and/or writing. Many assignments are constructed with the student offering a written response to a reading, a double whammy for those with language-based learning disabilities.

As an alternative, have students interpret nonverbal stimuli and respond in writing. Suggestions:

- Provide a cartoon as the stimulus on a vocabulary test. Students would respond using a specified number of terms.
- Have students research an image related to an era in history and respond to it in writing.

Having students interpret verbal material and provide a nonverbal response also works well. Suggestions:

- Have students depict the conflict in a novel through a drawing.
- Have students convey the theme of a novel through a photograph of their own or a collage of images they find in magazines.

WRITING TESTS—OVERVIEW

How a test is written or formatted can greatly impact a student's performance. When a student has difficulty interpreting a test, he often becomes nervous and confused. His self-confidence may get shaky, which can lead to many moments of self-doubt. When crafting a test, here are some common pitfalls and tips to consider:

- If you are writing by hand (not typing), be careful. Capital *B* can look a lot like a stick with a 3 next to it, or even a 13 if it's a math test. A Z can look like a 2. Mixing capital and lowercase letters can confuse certain students. Pick one style and stick with it. Work toward typing all your tests.
- If you use abbreviations not routinely used in class, write out the explanation on the test; if you just "tell" the students without writing it down, you're testing auditory attention and memory in addition to concepts and skills.
- Avoid hyphenating words at the end of a line. Some students will read more into this. If it's a math test, they might think the hyphen is a symbol for subtraction or a negative number.

- Be as specific as possible in setting your expectations. If you want a sentence, say so in writing. If you want a word or a number, say so. It's best to give an example as standardized tests do.
- Be consistent in the orientation of problems. If you begin writing problems horizontally, continue that way.
- Leave plenty of blank space between test items. This helps students with large handwriting who need more brainstorming and/or calculation space. I suggest allowing 2 to 3 inches for each multistep calculation. Providing a 3-inch left-hand margin can work well for calculation too. If you think this is unreasonable, try it five times and see if students improve.
- Leave a 2-inch space at the top and title it "Space for Splashdown" to encourage use of this test-taking strategy.
- On math tests, use as few periods and parentheses as necessary in directions. Save these symbols for their mathematical functions.
- Avoid using roman numerals unless your intent is to assess understanding of roman numerals. Students with learning problems often have difficulty differentiating left from right, so roman numerals are extremely confusing for them.
- Provide adequate context for fill-in-the-blank-type questions. This is important for foreign language since it's harder to pick up cues in an emerging language. Use at least two words on either side of a blank. If you must use fewer than two, provide the first two letters of the answer.
- Make sure maps have clear boundaries and are large enough to discern key features. For students with visual perceptual difficulties, lines indicating boundaries of countries and location of rivers can be very confusing, especially if they intersect. For these students, put an *R* on the line of the river. Put wavy lines to suggest waves in larger bodies of water.
- When asking students to match vocabulary items with a definition, be sure the definition contains words they already know.
- Use one side only. If students are flipping pages, working memory comes into play, as does attention. I advise students to remove the staple, separate the sheets, and look at the entire test, so number the pages too.
- Use at least size 12 font. I recommend Comic Sans or Arial.
- If you're using lined paper, don't underline items. Double lines confuse students with visual perceptual problems.

SUMMARY

The obvious intent of a test is to provide an opportunity for students to show what they know. The provision of accommodations helps them achieve this goal. In addition, the careful formatting of a test can help students show what they know. The impact of test format on student performance is significant. This is an area where teachers need to be aware of, and sensitive to, the clarity of presentation. The overview provided in this chapter can be a valuable tool for teachers developing tests.

One of the key elements involved in test format is the arrangement of material and the use of blank space. By placing word banks at the top of the page, allowing a generous amount of space for handwritten responses, and arranging multiple-choice answers vertically, the format of the test will lend itself to more successes and fewer obstacles.

Naturally, a number of students approach tests with a certain level of anxiety. By adding creative elements and even a bit of humor (e.g., cartoons), students may react differently.

Often, a student laments, "I studied hard for the test. I reviewed all the material. My parents quizzed me the night before, and I really knew it. With all that preparation, I still ended up with a C." There is a disconnect, and the student feels it. One possible explanation is that the test format did not work in his favor. Another potential reason for unexpected low scores on a test is the student's lack of test-taking tips. The following chapter offers techniques to remedy this situation.

9 Test Taking

Effective Tips for All

Many people will say that one of their nightmares involves a test-taking situation. That's not surprising, given the number of tests adults have taken in their lives and the emotional investment taking a test requires. Parents may comment that their child does not test well, but very few will say the opposite.

There are definite advantages to having a sure memory, steady nerves, and a good measure of self-confidence. Still, techniques are available to help improve the score of most students facing a test-taking situation. Consider the number of books on the market that claim to raise the score of students facing high-stakes tests, such as the SAT and ACT. Some simple techniques can hone this important skill. For example, knowing the testing terminology can clarify questions. Also, learning how to approach various question types (e.g., multiple choice) can give the student a clear advantage in this situation.

In the pages that follow, I have given certain test-taking strategies a name. Once a student has learned strategies, he will often reference them by name. Then, he will have an invisible coach, guiding him to use such techniques as "downsizing" or "splashdown." I imagine this is similar to recalling the advice of an athletic coach who advises a student to use certain plays in different situations. On some level, the student will sense that he is not in "the game" alone, whether that be on the field or at a table taking a test.

On a slightly different note, one of the accommodations I have facilitated over the years is scribing. Students with extremely labored writing or keyboarding dictate their responses to me. I record these responses directly on the test paper or type them on a word processor. The accommodation erases any negative effect writing difficulties would have on test performance but does require that the student have adequate verbal expressive skills and that he be seated next to me. This way, I can hear the responses, and he can see that I have recorded his answers as dictated. Students have a sense that they are working "with" me. This unanticipated benefit has been evident to me in the years I have scribed answers. Students perceive that they are not taking the test alone. They often check in to show me their grade on the test, saying, "Hey, Mrs. Martin, look what we got on the test!" I am quick to point out that the student earned the grade, and I simply acted as a scribe. Nevertheless, I hear how the relationship of teacher and student may have had a positive effect.

I encourage students to use the techniques offered in this chapter and to visualize the time when they learned them. This helps reinforce the notion that the students enter a test-taking situation with an invisible coach.

MUSIC AND TEST TAKING

A familiar and soothing piece of music seems to cross the boundaries of time and space. It can comfort an anxious student. Having the same physical environment (i.e., space and room) for testing isn't always possible, but melodies are available on a CD or an iPod with headphones or simply in the student's mind. Music can be the constant. By serving as a reminder of previous successful experiences in a different room, music may bolster confidence. A familiar piece can help students settle into the test-taking process, no matter where the assessment is located. I often use CDs with "relaxation" in the title. Strictly instrumental music (without lyrics) will not conflict with students who use a vocalization technique.

SENSORY FEEDBACK DURING TESTS

Occupational therapists will agree that allowing students to chew something that gives sensory feedback can calm them. I use Starburst candies and caramels. Because using candy in school is controversial, I chant, "Put the wrappers in the trash. Don't eat candy in class."

ANCHORS AND CLOZE

For multiple-choice questions, I call the first part of the question the "anchor." Sometimes, particularly for science tests, the anchor is long, for example,

Ecology is the study of the interaction of living organisms

I call the choices that complete the anchor "cloze responses." The cloze responses are usually the multiple-choice component and can also be quite long, again most often on science assessments, for example,

A. with each other and their habitat.

B. and their communities.

C. with each other and their physical environment.

D. and the food they eat.

Even if a student knows the content, retaining a long anchor in working memory while reading long cloze responses can be difficult. For this reason, I suggest the following:

When the anchor and/or the cloze responses are long, read the anchor along with each of the cloze responses, like this:

A. Ecology is the study of the interaction of living organisms with each other and their habitat.

B. Ecology is the study of the interaction of living organisms and their communities.

C. Ecology is the study of the interaction of living organisms with each other and their physical environment.

D. Ecology is the study of the interaction of living organisms and the food they eat.

This technique takes a bit longer but is likely to minimize the impact of a weak working memory. By the time the student gets to options C and D, the "anchor" may be clearer to him after multiple readings, an additional benefit of this test-taking strategy.

MANAGING COMPLETE SENTENCES

Using complete sentences can be frustrating for students with the following issues: test anxiety, word retrieval, and/or working memory. By the time they have written introductory words to set up a response, they may have forgotten the answer.

I advise students to leave space at the beginning of the question and jot the answers first. They can go back later and fill in the introductory words to complete the sentence. The amount of space they should leave at the beginning depends on the length of the setup. It might be a few inches or a line and a half.

Sample question:

> How much wood would a woodchuck chuck if a woodchuck could chuck wood?

Sample response in complete sentence form:

> First, students would write: _____
> about 3 pounds a day, assuming the wood is soft and the woodchuck has had good dental care and is fully motivated to chuck.

> Students would later fill in the front of the question with what I call the "setup":

> If a woodchuck could chuck wood, he or she would chuck . . .

"Splashdown" can help with this issue. This text-taking tip will be discussed later in this chapter.

Y, M, AND N

For multiple-choice questions, if a student doesn't recognize the correct answer, I encourage her to jot a letter to the right of the options. N stands for no, M stands for maybe, and Y stands for yes for example,

    A. blah blah blah N

    B. blih blah blih M

    C. blah blah blih N

    D. blih blah blah M

On this question, the student does not have a clear yes response, but since she has two Ms, she has a 50% chance of getting the correct answer. Having a clear method for comparing possible responses (options B and D) often helps with the final selection. This technique seems to allay some anxiety since it gives students an easy strategy to use when they are uncertain. I encourage students to record the Y because they may find two Ys, or two possible answers. They would then compare their selections to make a final choice.

CAUSE AND EFFECT

The word *effect*, usually used on history and science assessment, can cause students a range of troubles from spelling to meaning. I often substitute the word *outcome*.

Since many items involving cause and effect are assessing a student's mastery of sequence, it can help to substitute numbers instead. In the broadest context, any event could be viewed as a cause or an effect/outcome. This would be another good reason to use numbers.

"Cause" comes first, which becomes 1.

"Effect" (or outcome) comes next, which becomes 2.

DOWNSIZE

Particularly in math, if a student is stuck on a problem, I encourage "downsizing." The student's and my exchange goes something like this:

Lucy: What are you trying to do?

Student: Find 7/9% of 56.

Lucy: Which part of the problem is giving you trouble?

Student: The fraction and percent part.

Lucy: Which part of that is giving you trouble?

Student: I don't know how to do it.

The following is an example of "downsizing":

Lucy: What would you do if the numbers were simpler, like 1/2% of 10? How would you do this problem? (I now hold my breath and cross my fingers.)

Student: Oh, now I get it! (the usual response)

Lucy: So how will you do it?

Student: Explains method to me (and hears himself)

Lucy: Now take what you just told me and use it in the original problem. I think you can do it.

I may need to model downsizing a few times in a lesson. Then, I would expect the student to downsize on his own. Naturally, during an assessment, if the student offers the wrong explanation, I simply bite my tongue and later jot a note of the error in thinking. I comfort myself with the notion that, while he doesn't know the process, he is mastering a test-taking strategy.

TRUE-FALSE ADAPTATION

Taking a test in my room, a student described that when she sees underlined words, she sometimes gets "stuck" on them and cannot pull up the words she wants. This difficulty is likely related to word retrieval issues.

I covered up the underlined words with an index card and read each item aloud, substituting "blank" for the underlined words. She did well with this. Actually, I read the items aloud using a "fill in the blank" format, which worked perfectly for her. She did not "block" even once.

MULTISTEP DIRECTIONS

Many tests include items that require students to perform several different tasks. Here are a few examples:

1. Underline the adjectives, and circle the nouns they modify.

2. Define *republic*, and give an example of this type of government.

There is a simple strategy for responding to multistep directions: Number each required step. Usually, this involves identifying the verb that directs a response. For example:

     1   2

1. Underline the adjectives, and circle the nouns they modify.

     1   2

2. Define *republic*, and give an example of this type of government.

For greater reinforcement, students can jot the number of required responses next to the test item and then cross them off as completed. Numbering and crossing off requires students to be intentional and systematic, which may lead to fewer omitted steps and incomplete responses.

FEET FIRST

The value of attending to details cannot be overstated. This is particularly true on math tests involving units of measurement. Guide students to record the units of measurement (e.g., feet, inches, square meters) first. Advise them to move on to calculating the numeric portion of the response after they have recorded the unit of measurement.

There is a clear advantage to using this technique since the student does not have to change mental gears. All measurement. All calculation. Students with executive dysfunction and difficulties with cognitive flexibility will benefit significantly from this strategy.

On a test of area/perimeter, begin by filling in the units of measurement called for in the problem, for example,

1. _____ ft^2

2. _____ in

3. _____ m^2

Then, fill in the blanks by calculating the area or perimeter.

Tell your students to jump in feet first!

FIRST THE *YO*s, THEN THE *USTED*s

This tip will be most valuable for students who have trouble shifting gears or attending to visual detail or who simply struggle with foreign language or math computation.

When asked to complete sentences that require different verb-form endings, encourage struggling linguists to begin by completing all test items involving the first-person singular. Next, direct them to proceed to items involving the second-person singular, and so on. This is an efficient approach since the student will not have to change gears all the time. Students who have difficulty with cognitive flexibility will benefit from this tip.

This strategy will also work for math on a page of mixed computation problems. A student can first complete all the addition problems, then move on to the subtraction problems, and so forth.

WORD RETRIEVAL AND STAPLES

Some students struggle with word retrieval. They often have words on the tip of their tongue but just can't get them out. The deposit was made, the bank account is full, but they can't make a withdrawal. Anxiety can manifest in this type of blocking too. Picture this: You're at the podium ready to introduce a distinguished speaker, and his name suddenly vanishes from your mind. This is a classic situation of word-retrieval difficulty brought on by anxiety.

Often, the elusive word(s) can be found elsewhere on tests. Suggest to students that they unstaple the test if it has multiple pages. Encourage them to number the pages. Now, guide them to scan wording in other questions. Placing a hand or an index card on the page facilitates scanning. Quite frequently, you'll hear an "Aha!" as a student locates the needed word and puts in the correct form where needed. This strategy can be very effective.

Suggest this technique, and be sure your stapler is accessible!

"SPLASHDOWN"

A student came to take a test with extended time in my room. She said her head was "swirling with information," and she was nervous. I asked her if she wanted to "splash down" her ideas before she began.

Basically, to splash down means to jot quick notes to refer to throughout the test. Students perform splashdown prior to starting the test. I think of the process as emptying the mind of key information so the thoughts are on paper.

Once the student had splashed down, there was instant relief on her face. She was able to move through the detailed inquiries with confidence. Actually, she only needed to refer to her splashdown once.

"SPLASHDOWN" 2

A student came to my room to retake a foreign language test with extended time. On one portion of the test, he was asked to fill in a blank with one of two verbs. He was overwhelmed, made many self-deprecating remarks, and predicted failure. I encouraged him to use splashdown. To break inertia and provide structure, I made a blank grid for him, directing him to fill in pronouns and verb forms for each of the two verbs. He perked up and began to fill in the spaces. Even though he didn't know all of the verb forms, he realized that he knew some of them. Returning to the test paper, he was able to use the grid to fill in many of the blanks. His prediction was not accurate.

Teachers might want to provide blank (even unlined) sheets for students to splash down on. Collecting splashdown sheets to help diagnose problems can also be valuable. In foreign language, to facilitate splashdown on verb conjugation, it is valuable to provide blank grids for the student to use.

SIMPLY SCISSORS

A student took a test that required her to put events from her reading in the proper sequence. The events were listed in random order on the test paper, and she struggled to accomplish this task. This difficulty is common for students with learning disabilities.

I asked her if she would like to separate the events by cutting the paper; then, she could shuffle the events around freely on the desktop. Once she had arrived at her final sequence, she would simply number the events in sequence. She wanted to try it.

I photocopied the test and gave her scissors. When she was finished, I asked her if the cutting technique was helpful. She said it had made a *big* difference.

One of the roles of a learning specialist is that of a facilitator. I provided a space, offered an option, made a copy, and loaned scissors.

CBL—THREE-LETTER MAGIC

I was so prepared to take the written test at the Motor Vehicle Administration. I was confident, maybe overconfident. I had aced harder tests. I was on the brink of vehicular greatness. Then, it happened. The first question threw me an unexpected curve. I reread the item. I pondered different interpretations of the situation. All the choices seemed to fit. My face flushed, and my heart started racing. I came unraveled.

For many students, the first items of a test can affect the outcome. Even students who fall apart early on, however, can be straightened out.

Suggestions for Students

If you can't come up with an answer in 20 seconds, mark CBL (for come back later) in the margin. Move on to the next question. Do not worry if there are consecutive CBLs. As you move through the test, you will probably discover items that lead you to the answers for your CBLs.

Suggestions for Teachers

Review the first two items in each section with care. Directions, format, and language must be crystal clear. For example, "Fill in the blank" implies a line or an empty space will be provided for the answer. Some students get thrown off if they don't see the blank. This unexpected curve can set them on a downward spiral.

COUNT THE QUESTION MARKS

For multiple questions on tests, tell students to circle the question marks. Next, they should count them. Counting the question marks can help clarify how many answers are expected.

> Sample question based on *Anne Frank: The Diary of a Young Girl:*
>
> Why is Miep's cake such a treat? How does it also reveal rising tensions?
>
> The two question marks mean two separate answers are expected.

Remind students that noting the verbs in directions or questions can also provide them with information regarding the number of responses expected.

MANAGING HAND FATIGUE

I think about the multiple assessments and exams that students complete at the end of the year. I remember getting major hand fatigue from writing so much on such tests. Here are some suggestions to help manage hand fatigue:

1. Use rubber grips on pencils and pens. Some mechanical pencils come with them. Students of all ages seem to gravitate toward these pencils.

2. If students are working on a single sheet of paper, encourage them to put several sheets underneath it to soften the writing surface. This can make a big difference.

3. Permit the students to use a strikethrough rather than erase. When cleanly done, this type of correction should not be difficult for teachers to grade.

4. Pencil lead as soft as 0.9 mm doesn't break often but does smudge easily; however, 0.7 mm lead is a nice compromise.

5. Offer 20-second silent breaks for in-seat hand and arm stretches and shoulder shrugs. At first, students might feel a bit awkward, but

soon they will look forward to this mini respite. Little stretches can help reduce tension too.

MAKING SOMETHING OUT OF NOTHING

A student looks at a word. She says she has no idea what it means. Is she clueless? Not really. I encourage her to look at the word closely for possible hints. A good test-taking tip, this is especially valuable in grammar where prepositions and pronouns can be confused. When all else fails, look at what is given and "milk" it for all it's worth.

What could you get out of these words?

- Preposition—has something to do with *position*
- Pronoun—has something to do with *noun*
- Singular—has something to do with *single* or *one*
- Possessive—has something to do with *possess* or *ownership*
- Contraction—has something to do with *contract* or *squeeze*

Then, try combinations:

- Singular possessive
- Singular pronoun

WALLPAPER FOR OPEN-NOTE TESTS

When taking an open-note test, students spread out notes and books on the desktop. Given the limited space, many papers end up in a heap. Accessing the information is fairly haphazard as evidenced by the sound of frenzied flipping in the room. Encourage students to

- Number or letter pages involved in any packet or series of notes.
- Sit at a desk that faces the wall.
- Ask the teacher for permission to tape papers to the wall in front of them.
- Tape papers up in a sequence reflecting the sequence of information.

A Closer Look at Test Performance

Name _____ Date: _____

1. How long did you spend studying? (minutes, hours)

2. Did you study all in one night or in several nights?

3. How did you study? (check all that apply)

   _____ Read material silently   _____ Used a study guide made by the teacher

   _____ Read material out loud   _____ Copied notes over

   _____ Made flash cards   _____ Highlighted notes

   _____ Studied with another student   _____ Made a practice test

List any other ways you studied:

4. Did you attend any tutoring sessions?
   With your teacher? _____ How many times? _____
   With a private tutor? _____ How many times? _____

5. What did you study?
   Did you study the right material? _____ If not, what went wrong?

   Did you need to use notes? _____ Did you have good notes from which to study? _____
   If you didn't have good notes, what could you have done?

   Did you have all the handouts you needed to study? _____
   If you didn't have the right handouts, what could you have done instead?

6. How much do you participate in class?
   Put a dot on the line below to indicate how much.
   Never _____ A lot

7. Did you feel prepared to take the test? _____

8. How did you feel about the test? (Were you OK with the format, the content covered, and the length?) _____
   Put a dot on the line below to show how you felt about this test.
   Very easy _____ Average_____ Very hard

9. Did you have other tests on the same day?

   How many and what subject(s)?

10. How comfortable were you when taking the test?
    Put a dot on the line below to show how you felt about this test
    Very comfortable _____ Extremely nervous

11 Did you complete the test within the allotted time? _____

12. Did you have time to check your answers? _____

13. Did you skip any questions? _____

14. Were all the questions clear to you? _____

15. Did you have enough space or did you have to squish in the answers/work? _____

16. Summarize in a word or phrase what this test covered (for example: the title of the unit)

17. If you had an opportunity to take this test again, would you do anything differently?

If yes, what?

A CLOSER LOOK AT TEST PERFORMANCE

Many times, students prepare thoroughly, feel confident about the material, and use test-taking skills, yet the test results are disappointing. Students and parents lament that the test does not show what the student knows. It is important to look into the situation to see what went on. Where did things fall apart?

The student can fill out this form on his own or with a teacher, an advisor, or a learning specialist. I find "A Closer Look at Test Performance" to be a very useful tool in pinpointing a plan of action.

SUMMARY TIPS FOR TEST TAKERS

Splashdown

Jot notes in the margin about important information—you can refer to it later.

CBL

Jot these letters in the margin as a reminder to come back later if a fact or name is on the tip of your tongue.

Touch the Page

Use your finger, the end of a pencil, or an index card—this is *very* important.

Read Items Two or Three Times

Read items two or three times if you are confused.

Read Items Quietly to Yourself but Loud Enough to Hear Your Own Voice

Listening helps with comprehension.

Underline Key Parts of Directions

Underline key parts of directions, like *identify*, give an *example*, *explain*, *define*, or *predict*.

Number Multistep Directions

Look for verbs and check them off as you finish them.

Use a Marker to Check Work

A folded piece of colored paper—move it down the page as necessary—helps with focus and editing.

Ask for Help If You're Stuck

It never hurts to get clarification.

Downsize for Math

If you're stuck, set up a similar problem with smaller numbers. Then figure that problem out and apply techniques to the original problem.

SUMMARY

As with learning strategies, providing a name for test-taking techniques can improve student recall. Teachers can promote "splashdown" before tests are distributed. Formatting the test so a space for "splashdown" is designated would also go a long way to improving test-taking skills in students. "Splashdown" works very well on math tests and for students who have memory problems and/or anxiety.

If time management, anxiety, or word retrieval is an issue, students would benefit from using CBL. Sustaining momentum prevents some students from blocking, and one test item will not cause a downward spiral. Students just jot CBL after 20 seconds and move along.

Some students are challenged by the need to shift from one manner of thinking to another. The classic example is conjugating verbs in a foreign language where subjects are presented out of order as opposed to a formal conjugation. There is a simple solution: The student can do all items involving the same subject (e.g., first-person singular). This will require the student to note all similar pronouns and then answer accordingly. Remembering "first the *yo*s, then the *usted*s" can make a big difference in students' comfort, as well as their score.

In math, after completing a lengthy calculation of perimeter or area, it is easy to understand why students challenged by visual detail would simply jot the number and move on. If they jump in "feet first," however, they will begin by recording the units of measurement and then proceed to the calculations.

If points have been lost on previous tests for not answering all of the questions, students would be wise to "count the question marks." This simple strategy guides students to be more intentional in responding to several questions.

10 Self-Advocacy

The Path to Independence

From awareness to acceptance to advocacy, students who know and have come to terms with their strengths and weaknesses have achieved a great deal; nevertheless, there comes a time when even more is expected of them—speaking for themselves. Students' needs may be documented, and a number of plans may be developed to meet those needs; however, some teachers will need reminders about the plans in different settings. In elementary school and middle school years, learning specialists and parents share plans with teachers. They speak on behalf of the students. In high school and beyond, the students must develop the ability to speak for themselves.

Students are ready to advocate for themselves at different times. Timing can vary greatly. I have seen students who were ready and able to assume self-advocacy in the sixth grade. Others were reticent throughout high school. A number of factors may contribute to students' comfort, including personality (theirs and the teachers'/professors'), the school climate, and the students' verbal expressive capabilities.

When they are ready, students need to be taught self-advocacy skills and coached on how and when to use them. Some students may rely on written communication to convey their needs; others may prefer face-to-face conferences with their professors. By trying out different forms of communication, students will increase their comfort with self-advocacy. The learning specialist can act as a support person, as well as a coach. Developing scripts can be useful, as can role playing. In the *Journal of Learning Disabilities*, Patricia Phillips (1990) wrote about the positive effects of a self-advocacy plan for high school students with learning disabilities. The program led to a clearer understanding of the students as learners, an increased understanding of learning disabilities in general, and an emerging awareness of career and educational opportunities.

Many colleges and universities offer support in self-advocacy, usually through a department of disability support services. A number of useful Web sites for high school graduates can guide students along their path to independence and self-advocacy.

SCRIPTS FOR SELF-ADVOCATES

Encourage students to develop their own scripts. If writing is an area of difficulty, work alongside them to create the scripts. If all else fails, provide scripts and encourage them to paraphrase or memorize those that are relevant to their issues. Here are some examples:

"Mr./Mrs. Jones, may I speak with you privately? It will just take a minute."

1. "As you know, I have trouble with note taking. When someone uses Penned Notes, I'm able to concentrate on what is being said in class. I have the Penned Notes paper with me. Would you assign someone to take the notes? If you collect the yellow copy, I'll give it to the learning specialist, and he or she can make copies. Would you like any extra copies?"

2. "As you know, I use audio books for some of my reading assignments. I allow several weeks to get the material, so if you can tell me the reading assignments 3 weeks in advance, I'll be able to keep up with everyone else."

3. "As you know, I use an AlphaSmart for writing. I'd like to print my in-class writing in the learning specialist's office. Could you please dismiss me a few minutes early so I can do that and still get to my next class on time?"

4. "As you know, I qualify for extended time on tests and quizzes. My schedule is full today, but I'll be able to complete the test/quiz during study hall tomorrow. I'll plan to take it in the learning specialist's room and will arrange to have it put in your box when it is complete."

5. "As you know, I have trouble with organization. Will you help me develop a plan for the final project? If you can divide the project into "chunks" with me, I'll mark my assignment book with dates to 'check in' with you and show you my progress."

EMPHASIZE SOLUTION

Sometimes, I work with a student to develop scripts for self-advocacy. We role-play. If the student is comfortable with the diagnostic term, I encourage him to use it; if not, I supply a functional definition. The emphasis is on the solution, which comes in the form of an accommodation, a support, or strategies. Here are some examples:

I have dyslexia (difficulty reading), and that's why . . .

- I get books on tape. So, if you could give me a list of required readings for the next 2 months, I will order my tapes.
- I would prefer not to be called on to read aloud in class.

I have dysgraphia (difficulty writing), and that's why . . .

- I use an AlphaSmart/laptop for in-class writing and note taking.
- My IEP/Student Learning Plan has a spelling accommodation on it.

I have ADHD (trouble concentrating and sitting still), and that's why . . .

- I take my tests in a private setting.
- I get help with Penned Notes.
- I need to sit in the front row.

I have difficulty with processing speed (doing things as fast as my peers), and that's why . . .

- I will need double time on tests.
- I'd like to take my tests in the learning specialist's office.
- I can finish up during study hall or tomorrow during ____.
- The learning specialist will put my test in your mailbox. Is this arrangement OK with you?

The three magic words are *and that's why*. The two magic words for all of us are *thank you*.

PROMISES

Having disabilities makes life more complicated (and more interesting) for students with learning disabilities, as well as those around them. Even students who make every effort to succeed will occasionally disappoint themselves and their teachers. For those with disabilities, there seem to be more "bad" surprises than "good" ones. This pattern can understandably wear students down. It's one of the reasons I try to offer lots of encouragement and keep candy on hand. To limit disappointment, I caution students not to overcommit. I offer the following well-worn tenet:

Underpromise and overdeliver.

I explain that this will help remove some stress from the student. For example, a student may think the paper will be ready on Thursday but promise Friday. Also, I guide students to see that this will build trust with their teachers. For example, the teacher expects the paper on Friday but may receive it one day early.

BRIDGING THE GAP

Certain students are aware of their needs and accept their differences but aren't quite ready to speak up and advocate for themselves. Growth in this area can be facilitated by giving the student a prepared sheet that states frequently implemented accommodations and supports. The student checks off the supports that apply to her. This prepared sheet can offer a comfortable middle ground. The student participates but is not required to "speak up." By submitting the sheet over time, the student's comfort level is increased, and the script is memorized.

My IEP/Student Learning Plan says I do my best when

- I have extra time on tests. I may not finish in one class period, but I pledge to uphold the honor code.
- I take the test in a smaller environment. I choose to take the test in the learning specialist's room.
- I have support with note taking. Please assign someone to take Penned Notes for the class.
- I sit up front in class.
- I use a word processor or AlphaSmart for written work. I would like to get an AlphaSmart from the learning center. I would like to work on a computer in the learning specialist's room.

ADVOCACY SUPPORT IN COLLEGE

In college, students with documented learning disabilities may have an array of accommodations, as well as support. Trained personnel in the department of disability services can guide students in their efforts to become effective self-advocates. Students, however, must take the first step to connect with someone in the building. This could be through e-mail or in person. Students need to anticipate that the services will be provided only when an application for services has been submitted with the proper documentation. It will be important to know that the department needs time to receive the paperwork, review it, and finalize a plan. Then the benefits will be evident. If the department does not respond within 2 weeks, check on the status of the application for support services. While touring the campus initially, if a student is comfortable, it might be a good idea to drop by the building to familiarize him with the location of the building and perhaps pick up some information and forms. This will help give a sense as to the process, any deadlines, and the services available.

EXPLORING DEPARTMENT OF DISABILITY SERVICES

On a campus visit, checking out the department of disability services (often DDS) can yield a sense of familiarity with the location, the building, and some of the personnel. Still, for a number of schools, the procedures, policies, and support offerings may be overwhelming for both students and parents. Studying and evaluating these aspects of the DDS may be done at home. Virtually every institution of higher education will have a DDS that can be viewed online. Students should compare programs, ask questions through a contact, and download applications if interested. In addition, having an opportunity to speak directly with students who have used the services may prove valuable. Since information about DDS students is confidential, it will be necessary to obtain names and a release by working with counselors at the program. While in high school, parents and students are encouraged to seek out a college counselor familiar with DDS programs. Not every college counselor has such expertise. It will be well worth the time and effort invested to identify someone with such specialized knowledge. As an exercise in reviewing programs, check out the few college programs noted below. Understand that this is not an endorsement but rather a venue for exploration.

From the University of Maryland Web Site

http://www.counseling.umd.edu/DSS/

From the University of Arizona Web Site

http://www.salt.arizona.edu/

From the Adelphi University Web site

http://academics.adelphi.edu/ldprog

WHAT IF SELF-ADVOCACY DOESN'T WORK?

When a student understands his disability, accepts it, and explains his needs openly and clearly to educators, he has demonstrated remarkable maturity. He is to be commended; however, his achievement may not be recognized equally by all professors and teachers. Frankly, it is not a perfect world. Some educators are unaware of the vast progress that has been made in terms of "leveling the playing field" for students with disabilities. They may not know about the laws, Section 504, the Americans with Disabilities Act, and the Individuals with Disabilities Education Act. Teachers are very busy. They may appreciate a reminder. So the student should advocate for himself again, perhaps in another venue. If the contact was made by e-mail, a follow-up can be done in writing. If reminders do not bring about the desired response, it is best to turn this matter over to others. It is not the student's responsibility to address or correct such an impasse. If the necessary support or accommodations fail to be implemented, it is time to communicate with the school's administrators. At the high school level, the student could meet with the dean. At the college level, the DDS should become involved. Let others use their voice. A solution will be reached. In the meantime, I encourage the student to remain as positive and patient as possible, and move forward with other areas of study.

SUMMARY

Remember the three As: awareness, acceptance, and advocacy. The student's journey from the original evaluation has been remarkable. The readiness to self-advocate is rarely present until high school. At the college or university level, it become essential.

Students can work with teachers to develop a script. This will reinforce their self-awareness and enhance their self-confidence. The script will focus on the solution rather than the student's difficulties.

The development and delivery of the script can vary according to the student's needs. If recall problems are involved, it may take some time for the student to commit the script to memory. In this case, the student could submit the script in writing or e-mail it to a teacher. If the student has difficulty with written skills, the learning specialist or teacher could develop a script and ask the student to adjust it as needed. If verbal expression skills are weak or a student is highly anxious, face-to-face delivery would not be the best choice. Again, e-mail or written communication would work well. Confirming that the teacher received the communication will be vital in securing needed supports and accommodations.

Anticipating new teachers and professors, students should mark their calendars to "send out/deliver scripts." To avoid confusion, this should be done well in advance of the first class. Then, if there is any difficulty or confusion, an advisor or support person in disability services can be contacted.

Notes

Space for Your Own Ideas

Resources

Explore and Connect to Support

Information About Learning Disabilities: Web Links for Teachers and Families

ADDitude magazine
http://www.additudemag.com

All Kinds of Minds
http://www.allkindsofminds.org

AlphaSmart
http://www.alphasmart.com

Children and Adults with Attention-Deficit/Hyperactivity Disorder (CHADD)
http://www.chadd.org

Council of Exceptional Children's Division for Learning Disabilities (TeachingLD)
http://www.teachingld.org

Dragon NaturallySpeaking
http://www.nuance.com

Franklin Language Master
http://www.franklin.com

The International Dyslexia Association (IDA)
http://www.interdys.org

LDOnline
http://www.ldonline.org

Learning Disabilities Association of America
http://www.ldaamerica.org

Misunderstood Minds
http://www.pbs.org/wgbh/misunderstoodminds

National Center for Learning Disabilities
http://www.ncld.org

No Fear Shakespeare
http://nfs.sparknotes.com

Recording for the Blind and Dyslexic (RFB&D)
http://www.rfbd.org

SchwabLearning.org
http://www.schwablearning.org

The TechMatrix
http://www.techmatrix.org

References

Gardner, H. (1983). *Frames of mind: The theory of multiple intelligences*. New York: Basic Books.

Lavoie, R. (1989). *Understanding learning disabilities: How difficult can this be? The F.A.T. City Workshop* [Motion picture]. United States: PBS Video.

Phillips, P. (1990). A self-advocacy plan for high school students with learning disabilities: A comparative case study analysis of students', teachers', and parents' perception of program effects. *Journal of Learning Disabilities, 23,* 466–471.

Switzer, L. S (1985) Accepting the diagnosis: An educational intervention for parents of children with learning disabilities. *Journal of Learning Disabilities, 18,* 153–155.

Vail, Priscilla. (2007, December 5). *Learning styles and emotions*. Retrieved from the Schwab Learning Web site: http://www.schwablearning.org/articles.aspx?r=870

Index

CORWIN PRESS

The Corwin Press logo—a raven striding across an open book—represents the union of courage and learning. Corwin Press is committed to improving education for all learners by publishing books and other professional development resources for those serving the field of PreK–12 education. By providing practical, hands-on materials, Corwin Press continues to carry out the promise of its motto: **"Helping Educators Do Their Work Better."**